EVERYTHING BUT TYPICAL

EVERYTHING BUT TYPICAL

Influential Neurodivergent People Who Have Shaped the World

MARGEAUX WESTON

illustrated by
JESSICA CRUICKSHANK

BLOOMSBURY
CHILDREN'S BOOKS
NEW YORK LONDON OXFORD NEW DELHI SYDNEY

**Jarod, your support has helped me find
my own ways to shape the world**

BLOOMSBURY CHILDREN'S BOOKS
Bloomsbury Publishing Inc., part of Bloomsbury Publishing Plc
1359 Broadway, New York, NY 10018
50 Bedford Square, London, WC1B 3DP, UK
Bloomsbury Publishing Ireland Limited, 29 Earlsfort Terrace, Dublin 2, D02 AY28, Ireland

BLOOMSBURY, BLOOMSBURY CHILDREN'S BOOKS, and the Diana logo
are trademarks of Bloomsbury Publishing Plc

First published in the United States of America in September 2025
by Bloomsbury Children's Books

Bloomsbury books may be purchased for business or promotional use. For information on
bulk purchases please contact Macmillan Corporate and Premium Sales Department at
specialmarkets@macmillan.com

Library of Congress Cataloging-in-Publication Data available upon request
ISBN 978-1-5476-1411-0 (hardcover) • ISBN 978-1-5476-1413-4 (e-book)

Book design by Becky James
Typeset by Westchester Publishing Services
Printed and bound in China
2 4 6 8 10 9 7 5 3 1

To find out more about our authors and books visit www.bloomsbury.com
and sign up for our newsletters.
For product safety–related questions contact productsafety@bloomsbury.com.

CONTENTS

INTRODUCTION

There's a popular phrase we use in education about windows and mirrors. The original phrase, coined by the great educator Rudine Sims Bishop, refers to children needing books that serve as windows, mirrors, and sliding doors, to increase exposure to diversity. It's a call to action for everyone. Simply, it is that young people should have access to literature that provides windows for them to look at other cultures and ideas; mirrors, so they may see themselves within the pages of a book; and sliding doors to enter other worlds. As I was writing this book, I realized that I wanted to create the mirror I didn't have growing up. I wanted readers to see real neurodivergent people in a book and learn more about them living in their purpose and forging their own paths.

To do that, I had to show the many facets of neurodiversity. An umbrella description, "neurodiversity" (and related words like "neurodivergent") is a term that highlights many different processing types, learning abilities, and neurological differences. Some of them include ADHD, autism spectrum disorder, dyscalculia, dyslexia, Tourette's syndrome, bipolar disorder, synesthesia, dyspraxia, and sensory processing disorders. In short, neurodivergent people think differently than what is considered typical. As you can see, it's a pretty broad spectrum of differences, with people who have a variety of ability. There is no one type of neurodiverse person.

When I was younger, people associated autism with the character Raymond from the movie *Rain Man*. You may be a couple decades too young to remember the movie, but Raymond was a based on a real autistic man named Kim Peek. Peek was a savant, one who despite their mental disabilities demonstrates far above-average abilities. Peek was considered a megasavant because he had an amazing memory. It was reported that he could accurately remember the contents of nearly twelve thousand books. The movie was a huge success and catapulted Peek to fame. However, there were some negative consequences for the autistic community. For years after, many people assumed that *all* autistic people had some kind of genius ability or even superpower. Sounds unbelievable, right? Well, this was the eighties.

Autistic people were often judged by the things they could do (gifted in music, memory, or art) and just as quickly dismissed when they could not do those things. However, the rise of computers and the tech industry created another image of neurodiversity in the late nineties and early twenty-first century: that of the socially awkward, superintelligent computer guy.

The computer guy image was used in pop culture and created a new box for autistic people and other atypical thinkers. While many were praised for their gifts or intellect, others were ostracized for unpopular traits like stimming, tics, or hyperactivity: natural reflexes that made some neurotypical folks uncomfortable. And that was particularly true for people who faced discrimination from several directions, such as women, LGBTQIA+ people, and Black people, Indigenous people, and other people of color. If you didn't fit society's expectation of a neuro-atypical person, then where did you belong?

Fortunately, a sociologist was on the verge of something groundbreaking. She was working to create a word that encompassed the broad spectrum of differences, abilities, and achievements by neuro-atypical folks. Judy Singer, herself on the autism spectrum, developed the word "neurodiversity" as a term that recognizes that thinking differently is not a disability but a difference. Though the word was coined in 1998, it's taken a while for society to get on board.

Today you may see more neurodivergent characters in books and television. You may even see the term used more frequently and purposefully, but there is still room for improvement. One of the ways we can create more space for neurodiversity is by modeling, by exploring more lived experiences instead of solely creating texts centering on acceptance.

The people featured in this book not only serve as models but have also created their own definition of what neurodiversity is. They are high-flying Olympic greats, award-winning entertainers, and speed racers. They include women, BIPOC, and LGBTQIA+ people. Take Satoshi Tajiri, an autistic video game developer responsible for the megahit Pokémon. As a kid, Satoshi had an obsession with video games and bug collecting. He didn't do well in high school but went on to a technical college to study computer programming. Eventually Satoshi opened and created a multibillion-dollar company that combined two of his favorite things—collecting little bugs and video games—into what we know as Pokémon. Though Satoshi found classwork boring and eventually had to retake several classes, he persevered. Satoshi's obsession was actually intense concentration, something many neurodivergent folks can relate to. He was so focused on video games that he even took gaming systems apart to better understand them. He concentrated on merging the two things he loved and created a unique path to success that utilized his atypical brain.

This book is a collection of stories like Satoshi's: stories of everyday people who saw the world differently and conquered it in their own way. Tales of undeniable accomplishment, hope, and resilience—tales of people like you. My goal is for these twenty-three people to inspire you and help you to create your own path. These stories are for those who search for windows in books, so they may always consider what life is like in someone else's shoes. And of course, these stories are for those like me, who searched for mirrors inside books. As you read this book, I hope the reflection you see is filled with possibility and pride in discovering the many ways that you can create your own version of success in this world.

SIMONE BILES

Olympic Gymnast

March 14, 1997

Attention Deficit Hyperactivity Disorder

When Simone Biles arrived in Tokyo to compete on the US gymnastic team for the 2020 Summer Olympics, she felt the weight of the world on her shoulders. This was far from the first time her four-foot-eight frame had shouldered such a heavy load. She had been performing—and winning—as a gymnast since she was eight years old. At age nineteen, at the 2016 Summer Olympics in Rio de Janeiro, Brazil, she delivered a groundbreaking performance, dominating the individual competitions and leading Team USA in scoring. But this time, something felt different. It wasn't that the 2020 Olympics were actually being held a year late, in the summer of 2021, because of a global pandemic. It wasn't even the strict safety rules and procedures that had been implemented for athletes and fans to prevent the spread of COVID-19. Those things were different, but Simone couldn't shake the feeling that something else was just off.

Simone had struggled with crippling anxiety in the past and tried to sweep her worries aside, to focus on the routines she had executed flawlessly countless times before. But during her second day of competition, she experienced several mishaps and falls. It seemed Simone was struggling to carry the heavy weight of the world's expectations for her.

Perhaps the most frightening moment came when she was on the vault. She performed one-and-a-half twists, instead of the two-and-a-half twists she was supposed to, and nearly fell on her landing. The audience was shocked that Simone had not nailed her routine. Commentators noted that it looked like she got "lost" in the air. Simone spoke with her trainer as the small crowd watched in anticipation. She then left and came back in warm-up clothes, confusing fans who knew the competition was far from over. Instead of competing, Simone stood on the sidelines and cheered her teammates on throughout the rest of the meet. It wasn't until the next day that the world would find out that something was very wrong.

Simone had withdrawn from the competition, citing mental health issues.

She explained that she was experiencing the *twisties*, a psychological issue in which a gymnast becomes disoriented while performing. Losing awareness while twisting and turning through the air is extremely dangerous. In even the best of circumstances, gymnasts can seriously injure themselves with just one wrong move—and without mind and body working together perfectly, performing is incredibly risky.

Her decision was met almost immediately with criticism that she should've stuck it out. The world scrutinized the young Olympian, questioning her dedication to her sport and to her country. Although she had her share of vocal defenders—including fellow athletes who empathized with the pressure she'd been feeling, some of them gymnasts who spoke about their own experiences with the twisties—many critics suggested her mental health issues weren't real. From social media to TV's most controversial talking heads, everyone had an opinion about her actions, and the insults were severe. But Simone stood her ground.

As a world class athlete, she had dealt with critics many times before, most notably in 2016, shortly after a history-making performance at the Summer Olympics in Brazil. A few months after the games, she faced accusations of cheating when hackers exposed her private medical records. It wasn't that she had been caught doing something wrong, but that she took medicine to manage ADHD, attention deficit hyperactivity disorder. ADHD is a chronic condition with symptoms ranging from hyperactivity and impulsiveness to difficulty focusing. To defend her integrity, Simone publicly revealed her ADHD diagnosis. That didn't quiet all the critics, but Simone was used to both challenges and triumphs. She had bounced back from adversity countless times before, and to prove doubters wrong, Simone would propel herself to even greater heights.

Tiny Tumbler

Simone Biles was born in Columbus, Ohio. By the time she was three, Simone and her siblings had suffered from food insecurity and neglect and were in and out of foster homes. Soon, her maternal grandfather adopted Simone and her sister, and they moved in with him outside of Houston. She flourished in her new environment, especially when she was introduced to gymnastics at age six. She was a natural. From age six through thirteen, Simone trained to become an elite gymnast. This is also around the time she was diagnosed with ADHD. ADHD can make it difficult to learn and focus due to the brain's unique development. On the other hand, many people with ADHD have an uncanny ability to focus on activities or subjects that interest them.

At age fourteen she began competing nationally and she quickly made her mark. It wasn't long before she began competing internationally. But it wasn't all triumphs on the mat for Simone. During the 2013 US Classic, she had one of the worst performances of her career. She fell many times and finally twisted her ankle during the floor exercise. Simone was disappointed and unfocused, but she didn't give up. She realized that mental wellness, not just physical fitness, would be essential to success. Simone was handling her ADHD, but she would need to address her anxiety as well. Like Simone, many people who have ADHD also have an anxiety disorder. The challenges associated with ADHD can cause worry or stress, which is fuel for anxiety. It's one of the most common comorbidities of ADHD.

Simone soon consulted a sports psychologist to help her manage her anxiety and regain her confidence. Before long, she began to dominate the sport—her winning streak started at the 2016 Olympics and lasted for years, pushing her into the global spotlight. And while many were cheering on Simone and her teammates, others wanted to prove that Simone didn't belong at the top.

You Want to Know . . .

What does "comorbidity" mean?

Comorbidity is a term used when more than one condition occurs in the same patient. For example, if someone has autism and also has ADHD, ADHD and autism would be comorbidities. Comorbidities happen often with neurodivergent people. That means that if someone has one neurodiverse condition, they are more likely to have at least one other neurodiverse condition.

Nothing to Be Ashamed Of

In 2016, soon after Simone's fifth medal at the Rio Games, a hacker group accessed the personal medical records of Olympic athletes from the World Anti-Doping Agency database, an organization that ensures fairness at the Olympics by monitoring athletes for banned substances that improperly enhance their performance. They publicly circulated records for several athletes, including Simone, to question their success and discredit their hard work. The group uncovered that Simone used the prescription drug Ritalin, a stimulant that is prohibited by the World Anti-Doping Agency because, in neurotypical athletes, it can enhance focus and unfairly strengthen athletic performance. Little did the hacker group know that Simone didn't break any rules. Ritalin is an extremely common treatment for ADHD, and she'd received a Therapeutic Use Exemption permitting her to take the medication.

However, the world immediately began speculating about one of the world's top athlete's private medical information. Many wondered if her Ritalin prescription meant that she lived with ADHD. Some people thought that she couldn't have achieved her level of skill and success with a disorder that often affects focus. Others suggested that she should be ashamed of having a disorder.

Fortunately, Simone was ready to spring over this new hurdle. What she did next was nothing short of courageous: she stood up to the stigma of ADHD. Simone announced that she had ADHD and wasn't afraid for the world to know it. She declared that having the disorder and taking medicine for it was "nothing to be ashamed of."

Simone's boldness helped people see that living with ADHD doesn't mean that you can't be successful. It was the first time such a high profile athlete announced they were neurodivergent. Her simple statement opened doors for other neurodiverse people to proudly embrace their diagnoses, too.

We're Human, Too

In 2016 and again in 2021, Simone used her place on the world's biggest stage to speak out about centering her mental health. She insisted that athletes needed to protect their minds and bodies. They were not puppets, able to be pulled and pushed for entertainment. And in both instances, Simone changed things for athletes. It was often taboo to speak about mental health in sports. Not only did she address the topic head-on, she followed through with her actions, centering her own health—mentally and physically—and encouraging others to follow suit.

Neurodivergent athletes like Simone compete in tremendously high-pressure situations, and the stress and anxiety they face can make ADHD symptoms work overtime. Simone made every twist, turn, and jump look easy—until it no longer was. She overcame many obstacles to become the most decorated and celebrated American gymnast in history. And Simone became equally admired as a mental health advocate. She said, "We also have to focus on ourselves, because at the end of the day, we're human, too."

Since she was a child, Simone has been balancing life's highs and lows with agility, bravery, and poise. Her journey is a reminder that every setback is an opportunity to bounce back even stronger than before.

SATOSHI TAJIRI

Video Game Designer and
Creator of Pokémon

August 28, 1965

Autism Spectrum Disorder

Satoshi Tajiri had made a name for himself as a video game developer in the late 1980s. He'd also worked as a freelance writer reviewing arcade games. With razor focus and countless hours of work, in 1996, Satoshi was ready to launch his newest development, Pokémon, for the video game company Nintendo. Satoshi's game centered on imaginary creatures called Pocket Monsters, abbreviated as Pokémon. Players would take on the role of a Pokémon trainer, traveling the world of the game and collecting unique little monsters, and then training their Pokémon to battle with one another. The launch of Pokémon was Satoshi's life's work. It had cost him friends and coworkers, and nearly bankrupted him. He'd spend twenty-four hours working on the game and rest for twelve hours at a time. This game meant a lot to him; it was an idea born from a combination of vision and nostalgia.

As a child, he was an avid insect collector, spending hours looking for the smallest of creatures. Now he was a man who had created a game where users collected, trained, and traded little creatures. Would gamers enjoy collecting creatures as much as he did? When he'd first pitched the idea to Nintendo, they weren't too keen on the concept, but Satoshi's reputation was strong. They gave him a shot, and six years later he was ready to release his creatures to the world.

Pokémon was released in February 1996. This was a proud moment for Satoshi. He had finally stuck with something to fruition, a problem that held him back as a teenager. However, the moment quickly dulled. Media outlets paid little attention to Satoshi's new game. Game Boy, they said, was a dead console—the public had moved on to newer systems. Initial sales were very low. Satoshi worried that Nintendo would end their partnership.

It seemed that his years of sacrifice had been for nothing, but Satoshi wasn't ready to give up on his passion. Satoshi was on the autism spectrum. Autism spectrum disorder is a developmental difference that appears at a young age. Autism can impact areas of social interaction, communication skills, and cognitive function. Satoshi had challenges throughout school, but his super-sharp focus and attention to unique hobbies had brought him to this point and there was no turning back.

Dr. Bug

As a kid, Satoshi often got into trouble because he was too focused on his unique interests. Little did he know that he was building the foundation for the hugely successful video game company he would one day create. Growing up in rural Machida, Tokyo, Satoshi spent a lot of time digging through the earth and found bugs hiding in places most of us wouldn't notice. He enjoyed collecting insects, and his intense focus on this hobby lead to the nickname Dr. Bug. Dr. Bug may sound like a totally cool villain name, but it wasn't meant as much of a compliment. Satoshi spent a lot of time alone, completely focused on all things bugs. He imagined becoming an entomologist and being paid to study bugs full time. But soon things changed. Machida was growing and becoming more urban. The land he used to explore was transforming into the foundation for a city. And as school became cumbersome and boring, Satoshi pushed his entomology dreams away. He wasn't interested in his studies, and he struggled to follow through on tasks and complete big projects. As he entered his teen years, arcade and video games had his full attention. So much so that he often cut school to play games. He put bug collecting aside as he became more and more fascinated with the world of video games. Meanwhile, Satoshi was failing school and cutting classes to play video games. His parents assumed that these games were a bad influence on him and were worried about his future. Fortunately, Satoshi had a plan. He set his sights on becoming a video game developer and knew he'd need to succeed in high school to get there. His passion motivated him to earn his high school diploma and then a degree at a two-year technical program, where he majored in computer science. He went on to create a video game development company. Not bad for a kid who nearly failed high school, right? But Satoshi's wins wouldn't stop there.

Catch 'Em All

Despite its rocky start, sales of Pokémon slowly started to increase. Collecting Pocket Monsters, it turned out, was fun for all ages, and the game appealed especially to parents of young kids, who appreciated that it had minimal violence. (When Pokémon lose in battle, they faint instead of dying.) Another thing helped its sales—rumors. There were rumors in online gaming chats and blog posts about a hidden Pokémon who could only be accessed by exploiting errors in the game. Gamers argued about the validity of the rumor, with some claiming that there was no way it could be true. Finally, fans got their answer. A player had discovered a glitch that uncovered a new, mysterious monster. The rumor was true, and die-hard gamers flocked to buy the game, hoping to be one of the few who could access the hidden monster.

Eventually, Pokémon became a household name and is still popular today, thirty years later. Pokémon creatures have evolved into a highly collectible trading card game, have starred in TV shows and movies, have appeared on clothes and merchandise, and may even get their own theme park someday. Since its creation, the Pokémon company has averaged nearly $4 billion in annual sales and is one of the bestselling media franchises in history.

As for Satoshi, he's been named as one of the top one hundred game creators of all time. Like many people who are on the spectrum, diagnosed with autism spectrum disorder (ASD), Satoshi found success by focusing on things he was interested in. He started out as a kid who loved collecting bugs, grew into a teenager who loved playing video games, and became an adult who fused these two loves into one of the most creative, original, and well-loved video game franchises of all time. Satoshi's passion for Pokémon helped him turn his vision into a reality; and thanks to him, millions of people around the world love to "catch 'em all."

ARMANI WILLIAMS

NASCAR Driver

April 14, 2000

Autism Spectrum Disorder

From the time Armani was old enough to race Matchbox cars, he had spent every waking minute preparing for this day—his first NASCAR race. Armani showed an early interest in the mechanics of cars. He learned how to form words alongside learning about car parts. Soon, his family enrolled him in a go-kart racing school where Armani finally had the chance to get behind the wheel. They also took him to see professional car races. Watching the cars speed around the track, he visualized himself as one of the racers. He loved racing go-karts, but he had always dreamed of driving on the big speedway.

And now, after years of practice, Armani was sitting in his own race car at his first professional race. As he waited at the starting line, Armani visualized what was about to happen. He knew that as soon as the flagman gave the signal, each car would shoot forward at speeds above 120 miles per hour! Racing was dangerous, but as the start signal sounded, Armani reminded himself, *I'm prepared for this.*

Armani knew that, on the course, concentration was key. Race car drivers had to be quick thinking—able to react fast on the track—and have intense focus, paying attention to what's ahead of them, beside them, and behind them at all times. Fortunately, focusing on things of interest was one of Armani's greatest strengths. He thought about how his first race would go, imagining the sounds of tires burning rubber on the speedway, the supercharged speed he'd be going, and the possible challenges he might face. Armani felt prepared, but there was something else.

Competing in his first race meant a lot to Armani, but it was special to many others because it was the first time an openly autistic Black man was competing professionally. *Autistic.* Although he was diagnosed as a toddler, it wasn't until he was a preteen that he understood his disorder. He had gone through speech and occupational therapy from an early age to help him communicate and perform daily tasks. Now, at the Toyota 200, he would be representing autistic folks at the professional level in a dangerous sport. On that day, Armani was racing for more than just himself. If he failed, people may assume that autistic people just shouldn't race cars. But if he won, he would make history.

But Armani couldn't take too much time to think about the what-ifs—the race was on! Armani remembered his purpose and silently repeated, *I'm prepared for this.*

Hot Wheels

Armani didn't say much the first few years of life. He was diagnosed with autism spectrum disorder at two years old and was considered nonverbal. Some autistic people are nonverbal and others can communicate well. Armani's parents began to learn more about autism and how they could help Armani reach his full potential. They enlisted support from speech and occupational therapists, who helped Armani learn to communicate more clearly and to perform daily tasks like tying shoes, writing, and using scissors.

You want to know . . .

What is the autism "spectrum"?

The word "spectrum" refers to a range or a continuous sequence. You may hear people refer to autism as a spectrum disorder. This means that there is a wide variation in the severity and symptoms people may experience. If a person is on the autism spectrum, they are part of a large community of people with diverse characteristics, capabilities, and experiences.

His parents had learned that sometimes children with autism needed more time to complete tasks or extra support to reach a goal, but they also recognized something else. Armani's autism came with the ability to hyper focus—allowing him to pay attention to details that other kids his age missed. They didn't know it then, but Armani's ability to tune out distractions and concentrate intensely on specific tasks would give him a huge advantage in professional racing. Armani was nowhere near ready to get behind the wheel of a race car yet. First, he would need to master his first set of wheels—a bike.

By age six, Armani was still having a hard time riding his bike, but he was determined, and his parents knew he'd need support. They enrolled Armani into a two-week program to help autistic kids learn to ride bikes. Amazingly, Armani was zooming around by the end of the first day! Without any training wheels, Armani was pedaling, balancing, and speeding along. Armani could do hard things—he could reach goals while having an autism diagnosis. With his family's support and continual practice, Armani reached his goals. Nothing could slow him down now.

Knack for Speed

Armani's parents quickly realized their son had a knack for speed. He went from his bicycle to go-karts, from go-karts to a truck-racing series, and finally back to cars, his first love. At seventeen, Armani debuted at the Delaware Speedway in a Race 4 Autism speed car. He was careful to ease his way into the race. He drove fast but steady. As he drove, Armani got more comfortable with his speed. He lapped the course more quickly, whizzing past cars and maneuvering through the competition. Armani finished eleventh in his first race, conquering his lifelong dream of racing professionally and accelerating his goal of reaching the top spot.

Armani's races garnered attention for his skill and for raising awareness of autism. Armani's blue car was decorated with a Race 4 Autism sign along with small blue puzzle pieces—a common symbol of autism.

Fans and media wanted to hear his story. Armani explained how he got into racing and why driving professionally was so important to him. He said, "I wanted to prove to everyone that . . . autism can be a strength, not a weakness." His racing didn't only generate a greater understanding of autism, but it also broke barriers. Armani became NASCAR's first driver to talk about autism publicly. It was exactly what he had prepared for.

Shifting Gears

The race was on! Armani's car roared down the backstretch, maneuvering through the colorful cars. Some cars sped in front of him, whizzing by like a blur, while he zoomed past other drivers in a race to get to the finish line. By the end of the race, Armani gave a strong performance in the top twenty list. Armani and his supporters were proud of his debut and his history-making race. But Armani had learned something far more valuable than winning: he learned that he could bet on himself.

Although Armani has achieved his goal of becoming a professional race car driver—and before the age of twenty-five—he still has other plans. He plans to finish college, begin a career designing cars, and continue advocating for autism awareness and inclusion. His actions and persistence inspire others to keep pushing forward. Armani spent years preparing and gaining the tools to help him do whatever he set his mind to, showing everyone how multicapable the autistic community can be.

BILLIE EILISH

Singer

December 18, 2001

Tourette's Syndrome and Synesthesia

In November 2018, Billie Eilish took to Instagram to reveal something personal. The teenage pop star was used to performing in front of crowds, answering invasive questions from the media, and sharing details of her artistic life with curious fans. She was just sixteen years old, but Billie's career was already taking off: she'd just completed her second headlining concert tour, selling out venues across the country. Her music was wildly popular on streaming platforms, and she'd been nominated for the iHeartRadio Fan Fave New Artist award. As her popularity exploded, Billie had already shared so much of her young life with fans. Still, many pressed for more.

Several video compilations had been circulating online of Billie experiencing tics. Tics are unintentional, quick, repetitive movements that can happen randomly. The videos racked up millions of views and comments. Some people tuned in to mock her and leave cruel comments. Others expressed concern that Billie may have serious health issues. When she didn't immediately answer fans' comments about her health, many hypothesized that she was hiding something. Billie decided to address the rumors directly.

"I have diagnosed Tourette's . . ." the young singer revealed in a black-and-white, text-only post on her Instagram account.

25

Tourette's syndrome is a nervous system disorder involving tics. It can include both motor tics (repetitive, uncontrolled motions) and verbal tics (repetitive, unwanted sounds). In Billie's post, she explained that she'd taught herself ways to suppress her tics and reduce them. The singer also revealed that she hadn't planned to talk about her diagnosis, but the videos had forced her hand. Billie had already won over legions of fans with the authenticity and raw emotion of her music. It was fitting, then, for her to be just as authentic in her decision to share this part of herself with the world. Billie showed strength in speaking out amid negativity; however, it wasn't fair to push anyone—let alone a teenager—to reveal something that was so deeply personal. It was the first time Billie had to face the ugly side of stardom, but she'd learned early on not to let others' opinions define her. She knew that staying true to herself and her artistry was what made her captivating to fans. Billie marched to the beat of her own drum, and nothing would stop her rhythm.

Everything She Wanted

Billie Eilish Pirate Baird O'Connell was born in Los Angeles. Both her parents were actors and musicians. They encouraged Billie and her brother, Finneas, to explore the arts and embrace creativity while they were growing up.

Billie has shared that she, her brother, and her dad all have synesthesia, a condition that causes the brain to experience sensations in unique ways. People with synesthesia may notice crossover between senses like sight, sound, smell, taste, and touch. For example, sometimes when people with synesthesia hear music, they may actually see shapes or colors, connecting sound and sight together.

From a young age, Billie pursued acting, music, and art, but primarily she was a dancer. When Billie's dance teacher asked her and Finneas to write a song that Billie could use for choreography, Finneas suggested Billie try singing a song he had already written, "Ocean Eyes." Billie recorded the song, and it became a viral hit! She was only thirteen, but she quickly went on to break record after record. Her music topped the charts in the United States and in the United Kingdom. Before turning eighteen, Billie had received seven Grammy Awards, also becoming the youngest artist in Grammy history and the second to win in four specific categories: Song of the Year, Best New Artist, Record of the Year, and Album of the Year. She even went on to win two Best Original Song Oscars, one for the title song for the James Bond movie *No Time to Die* and another for "What Was I Made For?" from the movie *Barbie*.

While catapulting to musical stardom, Billie has also become known as one of the most creative artists in the business. She began trending for her fashion choices—oversized clothing, neon hues, and graffiti prints—meant for comfort and seemingly contradictory to the soft, though intense, ballads she was known for. Billie explained that her style was simply "expression without having to use words." She has a wholly original fashion sense, and her one of a kind looks always turn heads at award shows. Billie's authentic style and vision went far beyond the fashion world and into directing. Her music videos, like "Bored," are dreamy productions that stimulate the senses. Billie has credited her synesthesia with inspiring these dreamlike music videos. Synesthesia is associated with diverse points of creativity that activate the senses, sometimes more than one at a time. Billie's music videos are a feast for the senses.

Although Billie enjoyed artistic success, being in the spotlight has not always been easy for her. Regarding her style, she shockingly revealed that her choice to wear oversize clothes was also a defense mechanism—a way to prevent fans from commenting on her body. The revelation reminded fans of how cruel comments can make stars, even seemingly confident ones like Billie, self-conscious about their body image. Media and fans scrutinized her every move and commented on every aspect of her life; her popularity came at the expense of her privacy.

All the attention could be overwhelming for the teen star. She had weathered criticism about her talent, her looks, her style, her health conditions, and other aspects of her personal life. But Billie decided not to hide from critics—and in doing so, she became an even bigger inspiration to her fans. She leaned on her family for support, shared her struggles publicly, and encouraged others to seek help if they were overwhelmed, too. Billie didn't skip a beat, maintaining authenticity throughout controversy.

Happier Than Ever

When Billie revealed that she had Tourette's syndrome, she inspired many people to find out more about the disorder. Fans learned that there are hundreds of thousands of people who manage Tourette's syndrome. Journalists wrote about the diagnosis and applauded Billie for being brave and transparent. Billie's announcement put a face on the stigmas attached to Tourette's. At the same time, she emphasized that she didn't want people to think of her syndrome every time they thought of her—a message to which many people who are neurodivergent can relate.

In the years since her announcement, Billie has won nine Grammys and has appeared in film and television. She's proven that she's much more than her differences. She is brave, creative, and passionately human. Her music inspires people to feel deeply and soundly connect with her heart-wrenching tunes. Her differences have also given her the self-confidence to push boundaries and live her truth. Billie didn't let her Tourette's diagnosis, or the scrutiny of fans, stop her tempo. She bounced back, facing the world with renewed strength while marching to her own cadence of authenticity and resilience.

GRETA THUNBERG

Climate Activist

January 3, 2003

Autism Spectrum Disorder

In August 2019, sixteen-year-old Swedish activist Greta Thunberg arrived in New York City by boat after a fifteen-day journey. She was there to confront world leaders about the climate crisis. Greta understood that changes in weather and temperature were causing a big problem that needed immediate attention, and she could see that people in power weren't doing enough to fix it. So, she sailed from the United Kingdom to the United States to make her case to delegates from around the globe who were gathered at the United Nations Climate Action Summit.

Greta had chosen to travel by boat in protest of the harmful emissions caused by airplanes. She had made the dangerous journey with her father and a two-man crew, and rough weather had delayed her arrival. But her biggest obstacle of all was other people. Although she was a teenager, Greta had made quite the name for herself as a global climate activist, and many adults didn't like what she was doing. Naysayers lambasted her with cruel comments and news coverage that discredited her work. Greta appeared unfazed by her critics, affirming her intention to keep going: "Climate delayers want to shift the focus from the climate crisis to something else. I won't worry about that. I'll do what I need."

Many wondered why a teenager would spend her time embarking on such a tough journey. Activism, through rewarding, was not easy and required discipline and sacrifice. Just the fifteen-day voyage to New York had required Greta to sacrifice both time and comfort—she had to ride in a bumpy boat with no toilet across sometimes turbulent water—to show how serious she was. But when she arrived, Greta revealed that she had a superpower to help her with her activism: autism. Greta told the world that her autism diagnosis had beneffitted her, helping her get the support she needed and enabling her to understand herself better. She embraced being different and focused on her special interest—activism. She declared, "Given the right circumstances—being different is a superpower." In interviews she explained more about her autism diagnosis and how many people with autism had special interests. Though autism is a spectrum disorder, it is true that many people on the spectrum have unique hobbies and are able to intently focus on those interests, becoming experts in the things they love the most. They may also be more committed to their special interests, showing extreme persistence and determination for causes they love, than people not on the spectrum. It seemed that Greta had learned to manage her autism and use one of its symptoms—intense focus on special interests—for good.

The Young Activist

Greta learned about climate change at just eight years old. Climate change refers to long-term changes in weather patterns and temperature. These changes or shifts in patterns can be natural or caused by human activities. She learned that climate change was becoming harmful to humans, causing more severe storms and extreme temperatures. Greta also learned that there were things people could do to limit climate change, like burning less fossil fuel (like gas or oil) and recycling more. Greta's mind thought about all the ways humans were hurting the earth. She wanted to make sure everyone knew about the dangers of climate change and what needed to be done to stop it. But she wasn't sure her tiny voice could make an impact.

As Greta got older, she thought more and more about what she could do to solve such a big problem. She didn't understand why adults around her weren't taking it as seriously as she was. By age eleven, Greta was so worried that she stopped talking and eating much. She didn't want to go to school, and she stopped enjoying many of the things she used to. Around this time, she was diagnosed with autism spectrum disorder. The autism diagnosis helped Greta's parents understand her better and look for ways to help her move forward. Fortunately, Greta's family encouraged her to get more active in climate activism. They knew how important the climate was to her and that activism made her happy.

In 2018, at just fifteen years old, Greta took bold action. She made a huge sign that read School Strike for Climate, skipped school, and sat down with her sign outside of the Swedish government headquarters. She did this every Friday, skipping school against her parents' wishes. Greta hoped that politicians would take notice and begin working to end climate change. Greta was greatly inspired by the teen activists in Florida who were protesting gun violence after another school shooting claimed the lives of their friends and peers. As Greta had anticipated, the Swedish media soon noticed her protest and word spread globally. Soon, thousands of students from around the world joined her #FridaysForFuture movement, skipping school each week in protest of climate change. Many people were surprised that one teen had sparked an international protest, but Greta knew that she wasn't alone. She amassed a large following on social media, and inspired other teenagers who felt drawn to her cause and determined to enact change. Greta was officially an international climate activist. It was her first major protest, but Greta knew that it wouldn't be her last.

Climate Change Legend

While Greta inspired teens across the world to get active in climate change activism, she was clear about those who had inspired her. In addition to the gun violence protests in Florida, she credited a civil rights legend who had sparked a national movement: Rosa Parks. In 1955, Rosa Parks had changed history by refusing to comply with a law that segregated Black people on public buses during the US Civil Rights Movement in the 1950s and 60s. Now, Rosa's bold refusal had inspired Greta to take a similar stand.

The success of the Fridays for Future protests motivated Greta to think bigger—and soon she began planning her transatlantic voyage, where she would confront not just her own country's government but leaders from all over the world. In New York, she fearlessly demanded change—change that was needed *now*. Although some dismissed her, many more were inspired by her, especially other teenagers. Using her superpower, Greta galvanized people across the globe to get more serious about solving climate change, but she knows there's still much more to do. Greta has continued her climate change work and has also spoken out about injustices across the world. Through her Fridays for Future movement, she's met other like-minded activists, some with autism, who have joined her cause. Greta has built a movement that is inclusive to all. She not only uses her superpower but also recognizes that we all have superpowers that can help shape the world!

You Want to Know . . .

How do you know if you are neurodivergent?

Many people who are neurodivergent have been diagnosed with a disorder or developmental delay by a doctor. For others, mainly adults, they may believe they have behaviors that are outside what is considered the norm and self-diagnose themselves. If you think you may be neurodivergent, it's important to ask a trusted adult for support.

AMANDA GORMAN

Poet

March 7, 1998

Auditory Processing Disorder

When Amanda stepped to the podium at the 2021 US presidential inauguration, the whole world was watching. It wasn't just the excitement of swearing in a new American president, or that Amanda would be the youngest poet to read at a presidential inauguration in US history. The stakes felt much higher than at other inaugurations. A historic horror had happened just days before, and the country was more divided than ever.

The date was January 20, 2021, and just two weeks earlier, on January 6, disgruntled supporters of President Donald Trump had stormed the US Capitol. Months earlier, Joe Biden had defeated Donald Trump in the 2020 presidential election, and now Biden was about to officially take office. But the mob, through intimidation and violence, had come to stop the peaceful transfer of power from one president to the next. Hundreds of people forced their way into the Capitol, injuring peacekeepers and bystanders, while the world watched in horror. After several hours of chaos, the trespassers were finally removed from the building and order was restored. But in the days that followed, the tension between those who believed Donald Trump should have won and those who supported the election of President Joe Biden was still in the air.

As Biden took his presidential oath on the very same steps where violence had taken place, Amanda, the twenty-two-year-old poet, was faced with a problem: How could her words help to mend the tension in the country? She had already planned to read "The Hill We Climb," a poem that envisions a safe and free America, dismantling the legacy of fear and intimidation experienced by many people of color; but Amanda knew the nation needed something more, something that would unite everyone once again. She revised the poem to address the recent storming of the Capitol. But would people still like it? For Amanda, the title of her poem was more than just a metaphor for the country. She'd had to climb a hill of her own to get to this moment. Just a few years ago, Amanda had a speech impediment caused by an auditory disorder. Even as she became known for her powerful poetry, Amanda still had trouble saying certain sounds. On that day, January 20, she was expected to deliver a flawless performance on a national stage—something she'd grown into doing quite well—but the pressure from the dangerous tension across the nation threatened her confidence. Amanda recited a mantra to herself, *I'm the daughter of Black writers. We're descended from freedom fighters who broke through chains and changed the world. They call me.* With renewed strength, she walked up to the podium and onto the world stage.

For the Love of Words

As a kindergartner, Amanda was diagnosed with an auditory processing disorder. Auditory processing disorders can make it difficult to understand what people are saying. This isn't a hearing problem and doesn't involve any damage to the ear. It's an issue with the part of the brain that processes sounds. Auditory processing disorders can impact people in different ways. For example, some people with auditory processing issues can't differentiate between separate sounds, while others have trouble recalling what they've heard.

For Amanda, the auditory processing disorder affected her speech, making it challenging for her to pronounce certain words. Still, Amanda had a love for words. She learned to read later than other kids her age, but once she knew how, she was hooked! Amanda found comfort in exploring other worlds through books. Books allowed her to think beyond her words. Her auditory processing disorder made it harder for her to express herself to those around her, but reading helped her find her voice.

Amanda's newfound passion for words gave her the strength to traverse through any obstacles she faced. "My challenges were always, just for me, something that was reality. But I knew I had strengths, too, especially with words and writing," she said. Over time, Amanda began writing her own stories. By third grade, Amanda became interested in poetry. She loved the way poetry expressed ideas. She read the books and poetry of Maya Angelou and became particularly inspired by Maya's autobiography *I Know Why the Caged Bird Sings*. As a child, Maya was mute for a period of time after a tragic event. For years, she did not speak up for herself. Amanda could relate: "I felt like Maya was me growing up. She overcame years of not speaking up for herself, all for the love of poetry."

Youth Poet Laureate

Amanda's poetry garnered the attention of her teachers and even attracted fans in literary circles around her hometown of Los Angeles. In 2014, she applied to become the Los Angeles Youth Poet Laureate, a distinguished title given to one student in the entire city to share and promote their poetry, and sometimes to write and read poems at official events. And she won! This huge accomplishment led to her work being read by more people across the nation. At just sixteen, Amanda was quickly becoming a household name. Through the Los Angeles Youth Poet

Laureate program, she published her first book of poetry, *The One for Whom Food Is Not Enough*. As her work became more popular, Amanda continued to climb toward even greater heights. In 2017, she was named the first ever National Youth Poet Laureate, and in 2020 she not only graduated from Harvard but also gave the virtual commencement speech that year. From there, her star only continued to rise—until, in 2021, she found herself on the steps of the US Capitol to celebrate the inauguration of the forty-sixth president of the United States.

The Hill We Climb

The air was brisk and heavy as Amanda stood at the podium. She took a few moments to begin, appreciating the applause of the crowd. She not only addressed the audience seated in front of her but also the world. She spoke about democracy and hope for a better future. She spoke about putting differences aside and embracing diversity. Amanda's words, though picked especially for the inauguration, were also deeply personal, reflective of her journey to adulthood. As a child who struggled to articulate her thoughts, Amanda faced adversity. She could have easily given up her love of words for something much easier to conquer. But she kept climbing. As Amanda stood on Capitol Hill, it was clear that her hard work had paid off. Amanda's inaugural poem touched those who heard it and was replayed and printed for the world to read. In the final words of her poem, she called on all of us to be brave enough to *see* the light and to *be* the light. Her poetry offered hope to those who are fighting for truth and those who are finding their voice.

JASON ARDAY, PHD

Professor

May 9, 1985

Autism Spectrum Disorder

Jason Arday has always believed he can achieve the impossible. He once ran thirty marathons in just thirty-five days, raising over six million dollars for charities around his hometown, London. And in 2023, at just thirty-seven years old, he became the youngest Black professor at the prestigious Cambridge University in the United Kingdom. But his most impossible achievement of all may have been learning to read and speak.

When Jason was just three years old, doctors told his parents that he was autistic and nonverbal. They did not believe he would ever be able to speak or learn how to read. After years of family support and therapy, Jason proved doctors and specialists wrong. He said his first words at age eleven and began to read and write at age eighteen. Medical professionals could not believe how much Jason had changed in such a short time. However, autism is a permanent diagnosis, something Jason would have to manage for the rest of his life. He knew that he'd have to face more challenges, but he'd already proven that he could achieve the unthinkable.

Underestimated

"Not many teachers at school had any belief in me," Jason revealed during an interview. When doctors diagnosed Jason with autism spectrum disorder, they also informed his parents that he had global developmental delay. Autism affects communication, processing, and social interaction. A global developmental delay means that a child will take longer than average to reach development milestones. Things like walking, talking, and learning new skills would happen more slowly, or never happen at all.

Doctors told his parents that Jason would struggle throughout life and would need assisted living when he became an adult. While Jason's parents accepted his diagnosis, they believed he would exceed the doctors' expectations. They taught him sign language to help him communicate nonverbally. His mother, Gifty, continually told her son that he would do great things. She introduced him to music and encouraged him to use sound to make sense of the world around him. Jason could not speak, read, or write, but he began to love music.

Gifty was an anti-racist activist who regularly took Jason with her to protests and marches for justice. Jason listened to the crowds voice their concerns and learned how to advocate for change. His parents had walls filled with books, just waiting for Jason to explore. He also received professional support from speech and occupational therapists. Words, sounds, knowledge, and love were always around him. At age eleven Jason said a simple word that changed his life: "hello." Jason was able to speak!

It Won't Always Be Like This

Once Jason began speaking, he was ready to tackle another challenge: reading and writing. Jason recalled that, before he began speaking, reading, and writing, his mind worked like a flip-book with moving pictures. He explained, "When you're cognitively impaired, you make sense of things in different ways." Jason had learned to use images to understand what was going around him, and he would use this same technique to work toward his next goal. At age eighteen, Jason once again did what he'd been told was impossible—he began to read and write.

Now, Jason was talking, reading, and writing with fervor. No one had thought Jason could accomplish this, but he wasn't finished defying expectations. He successfully finished high school and turned his focus to college. He didn't just complete his undergraduate degree, but he also earned a master's degree and applied to pursue a doctorate degree—the highest educational level one can achieve. His advanced studies required hard work and lots of reading and writing, but fitting in was even harder. Jason worried that if people knew he had only learned to read and write at eighteen, they would think he didn't deserve to be in a high-level academic program at all. To avoid standing out among his peers, he "masked." Masking is something neurodivergent people do to hide their neurodivergent traits or differences. For example, some people with autism have trouble maintaining eye contact, but they might mask by forcing themselves to look others in the eye even though it makes them uncomfortable. At school, Jason masked by maintaining eye contact, adapting his tone of voice, and matching others' body language. Masking may have caused him discomfort, but he did not want to feel like an outsider again.

Jason studied through the night and sacrificed time with family to finish school. However, his hard work paid off when he earned his doctoral degree in 2016! Jason attributes his success to the people who supported him when others had given up on him. But he also believed in himself and that he could achieve the impossible. When things got tough, Jason recited a mantra that kept him positive and focused: *It won't always be like this.*

The Professor

After Jason received his doctorate degree, he worked as a university professor, where he focused on diversity and education. He wrote scholarly articles on the topic and became one of the experts in his field. His work was so impressive that he was hired at Cambridge University, one of the top colleges in the world, where he continues to teach, research, and publish his work.

As the youngest Black professor at Cambridge, Jason has forged a path that seemed unthinkable when he was first diagnosed with autism and global developmental delay. His achievements as a neurodivergent person of color are groundbreaking, providing a beacon for other autistic scholars.

Jason's ascent to greatness also shows ways to help people with autism thrive. He benefited from the love and encouragement of his family and from early intervention and support from therapists and professionals. Although some nonverbal people on the autism spectrum remain nonverbal well into adulthood, others eventually learn how to communicate verbally, by sign language, or through specialized electronic devices called augmentative and alternative communication devices. These devices act as tools to help nonverbal people communicate by pressing buttons or pictures that correspond to their needs. Advances in technology are broadening the communication possibilities for many people. Access to the right support can help neurodivergent people reach their full potential, but another key is reducing stigmas around neurodivergence. Although Jason masked his neurodivergence for years, more recently, Jason has begun to talk about autism and navigating the world with neurodivergence. By talking about the way his mind works, Jason is helping to normalize differences in intellectual ability and processing.

Jason's amazing story—from learning to talk at eleven, to reading and writing at eighteen, to finding success in a career path where mastery of reading and writing is so essential—serves as inspiration to anyone who has ever been told that their future will be limited. Like Jason, we all have the potential to achieve the impossible—especially when we get the support we need to flourish.

OCTAVIA E. BUTLER

Author

June 22, 1947–February 24, 2006

Dyslexia

When Octavia Butler was awarded a prestigious MacArthur Foundation grant in June 1995, she could not believe it. The MacArthur grant was often called the "genius grant," and Octavia did not believe she was a genius. But MacArthur fellows, the title given to those who win the award, are nominated by their peers—those who worked alongside them and admire their achievements. The fellows are diverse, hailing from various industries. They are scientists, historians, and prolific thought leaders. They are musicians, writers, and dynamic artists. But there had never been a Black science fiction writer—until Octavia.

By the time Octavia won the MacArthur grant, her books were pretty popular. But just a few years before, not many people knew Octavia's name, let alone considered her a genius. During the 1970s, when Octavia began writing uncanny stories, science fiction was dominated by white male writers. There were very few sci-fi books published by women and people of color. Luckily, Octavia had an amazing imagination—and a strong belief that she'd become a successful writer. She would wake up early to write her stories before heading to work. She had several odd jobs, including one as a dishwasher and another as a potato chip inspector. Octavia didn't like these jobs, but they paid the bills and allowed her enough time to think about far-out stories and imagine her future as a writer. Finally, after her work was rejected by several publishing houses, her first book, *Patternmaster,* was acquired and published in 1976. The book centers on a future where telepaths are the ruling class. Octavia was happy that she finally sold a book, but she didn't get paid much money. She would still have to work hard and write more books to earn a living. She didn't imagine that she would one day be crowned a "genius."

When Octavia was a young girl, not many people imagined that she could have a career as a writer—and not just because, as her Aunt Hazel told her, Black people couldn't be writers. Octavia was dyslexic, a learning disability that affects reading, spelling, and writing. But despite the challenges she faced, Octavia believed in her incredible imagination—an imagination amazing enough not only to write herself into the genre of science fiction but to write stories unlike any the world had ever seen.

Writing Herself into the Story

As a child, Octavia Butler had trouble relating to many of the books her teachers gave her. She grew up in the 1950s when most popular books featured characters that did not look like her. She was also bored with the realistic, dull settings that suppressed her imagination. But boredom wasn't the only thing slowing down Octavia's reading. Her teachers thought she was lazy, withdrawn, and uninterested in completing her assignments. The truth was that Octavia had undiagnosed dyslexia. It often took her longer to complete reading assignments as she processed word sounds and letters. She developed a strategy to "listen" to each word in her head so she could better understand the meaning. The process was slower but allowed her to understand how words were used to convey emotions and paint pictures. Although her teachers were not encouraging, reading at a slower pace did not stop Octavia from imagining new worlds.

She longed for books featuring Black characters with superpowers and futuristic, far-out settings. Her mom took her to get a library card, and Octavia began going often, taking solace in the fantastic worlds within books. She'd found science fiction—and she was hooked! She even called the library her second home. Octavia hadn't made many friends in school, but at the library she quickly found a sense of belonging through the fascinating stories and powerful words she read.

Meanwhile, science fiction was exploding across the country with TV shows like *The Twilight Zone* and *Star Trek* dominating the airways. The media was also building public support for space exploration through education because of the Space Race, a competition between America and Russia on who would reach the moon first. As her teachers began talking more about space travel and the future, Octavia dreamed of touching the stars and searched for more stories about uncharted worlds.

By the time Octavia was in junior high, she loved stories about the future— uncanny aliens and humanlike creatures with extraordinary abilities. But in all the science fiction she read, she did not find any Black characters. So, she wrote her own. She put her imagination to use—incorporating Black people in her stories, and aliens, and people with superhuman abilities. She loved characters who were different, just like she felt at school. When Octavia shared her stories, many of her teachers thought they were plagiarized because they were so out of this world. But one teacher encouraged her to send her work to magazines. He believed Octavia was talented enough to publish work that could be read around the world. At thirteen, Octavia submitted a story to a science fiction magazine for the first time. Although she never received confirmation from the magazine, Octavia kept imagining and kept writing.

Persistence

Octavia often wrote affirmations to herself, like, "I shall be a bestselling writer. . . . So be it! See to it!" These notes helped her remember her purpose when publishers rejected her work or when she faced challenges as a dyslexic author. These affirmations strengthened her belief that success was possible.

She continued to practice writing, and she took every opportunity to learn more. Eventually, she took college courses in writing. Soon after college, Octavia sold her first two science fiction short stories!

Octavia went on to write several books. One of her most famous novels, *Kindred*, tells the story of a young Black woman writer who mysteriously travels back and forth in time. In the past, the main character faces the dangers of life as an enslaved woman in the antebellum South. Published in 1979, the book showcased the cruelties of American slavery.

By the early nineties, Octavia's work was being celebrated. She won two of the top awards in science fiction, the Nebula and the Hugo. She became a pioneer in science fiction, opening the door for many other female and Black writers.

In 2006, Octavia Butler passed away suddenly, but her work lives on. In 2020, one of her affirmations finally became reality when her book *The Parable of the Sower* hit *The New York Times* bestseller list—nearly thirty years after it was published! Her books have even become TV shows and are set to become films. The young girl who once felt like an outsider grew up to be a genius, creating alternate futures and stunning worlds where Black people, uncanny superhumans, and colorful creatures exist. Despite the challenges Octavia faced, she never stopped imagining. And her stories not only transformed the genre of science fiction, they captivated the world.

CAMONGHNE FELIX

Essayist, Poet, and Political Strategist

January 15, 1992

Dyscalculia and Bipolar Disorder

Working as both a poet and political strategist may seem like an unusual pairing. One deals with imagery and creative descriptions while the other centers hard-hitting facts. But for Camonghne Felix, both roles give her the opportunity to inspire others through her words and ideas. She writes stories that reflect her life and challenge readers to use their voice to advocate for racial justice and social change.

Camonghne Felix has made a name for herself in the literary world. Her work has been nominated for prestigious awards and has appeared in magazines like *Teen Vogue* and *Poetry Magazine*. While building her profile as a creative writer, Camonghne has also made a name for herself in the fast-paced world of politics. As a political strategist, she develops messages and campaigns to help candidates win elections—a job that draws on her creative writing skill set and her journalistic expertise. When asked about how she balances writing for different audiences, Camonghne says, "To do my best work in politics, I have to think poetically. And to do my best work in poetry, I have to think politically."

In 2023, Camonghne released her memoir, *Dyscalculia*, which explored her lifelong challenges with being neurodiverse, her experience with disappointment and pain, and her misunderstanding—or miscalculation—of relationships. The book's title is a nod to Camonghne's learning disorder, dyscalculia, which inhibits one's math abilities. The book was listed as one of the Best Books of 2023 by *Time* magazine and the Chicago Public Library. While the author had been recognized for her powerful writing before, this book was her most personal work yet, exposing her challenges growing up neurodivergent and maintaining relationships with friends and loved ones.

Camonghne focused on using her words to incite change, a skill that she'd developed as a kid. She spoke out passionately about creating a better world. But just years before, Camonghne struggled in finding ways to balance neurodivergence with expectations from the people around her. Having an atypical brain in a typical world proved to be a challenge. Camonghne always had a way with words, but other parts of her life didn't add up so easily.

Long Division

At around eight years old, Camonghne stopped being able to do math. Her mom noticed that she had trouble completing her long division homework. Camonghne hadn't just forgotten a few steps or missed a few questions. She seemed to have forgotten every math concept she'd learned—math was like a foreign language. Her teacher sent home notes about her lack of focus in class, and she got in trouble for submitting incorrect homework. Like any concerned parent, her mother looked for ways to help her. She offered her educational computer games and encouraged her to rediscover the fun in math. But Camonghne's sudden math problems remained a mystery. Just the year before, she had been a good math student, frequently using mental math and excelling in her class. Something had changed.

As math classes got harder, Camonghne's mom fought harder to find solutions. Soon, she'd find out that the reason for her daughter's rapid learning regression was because of trauma. Trauma is an experience that hurts someone physically or emotionally. Trauma has different effects on different people. It can make them sad or confused, or affect memory. For Camonghne, trauma affected her capacity to understand math concepts, and eventually began affecting her self-esteem. Camonghne went to doctors and got therapy to help her heal from trauma, but her family still didn't have a name for the changes she was experiencing.

Unfortunately, her challenges with math would persist even though she got extra tutoring and attention to help her regain math skills. Throughout high school, teachers thought she just didn't want to learn. She felt left behind and changed high schools a few times in search of the right fit.

Finally, Camonghne found an educational program that fit her needs. Through hard work, she excelled and graduated from high school. But she still faced the effects of the trauma that happened to her when she was a young girl. She sought out help and was diagnosed with bipolar II, a mood disorder. Bipolar II disorder can cause long periods of depression and sudden, severe mood changes. Identifying her bipolar II disorder helped Camonghne put things together, however, she still couldn't solve her math challenges.

Camonghne spent time researching comorbidities, medical conditions that exist alongside another diagnosis. She learned that many people diagnosed with bipolar disorder also struggled with math. She learned about dyscalculia, which impairs a person's ability to learn number-related concepts or problem solve. It affects numbers just like dyslexia affects letters. Dyscalculia described the exact challenges she'd faced since the second grade. Her doctor confirmed that she likely had dyscalculia. Although it was frustrating to have waited so long for this answer, things finally began to add up. Armed with a name for her challenges and a desire to change the world through her words, Camonghne set out to shake things up.

Moving Forward

Camonghne has written everything from poetry to political speeches. She has participated in poetry festivals and has performed her poetry for national audiences. In 2019, her debut poetry collection, *Build Yourself a Boat*, was nominated for a National Book Award and a Lambda Literary Award, which honors LGBTQ+ literature. Her poems have been featured in major outlets from *Glamour* to *The New Yorker*.

In addition to writing poetry, Camonghne worked in political communications. She became the official speechwriter for former New York governor Andrew Cuomo. She was the first Black woman and youngest person to hold that position. In 2020, she joined Elizabeth Warren's presidential campaign. As a political writer and strategist, Camonghne has been able to advocate for causes she believes in and use words to ignite change.

Although it took a while for Camonghne to solve her math problems, now she channels that experience into bringing awareness to bipolar disorder and dyscalculia. She candidly shares her experience as a neurodivergent Black woman shaping the world through writing and social justice. In an interview, she explained that her goal was to "make the world better for people who have less privilege than I do. I do that through working in politics and through writing poetry."

No matter what she's writing, Camonghne is working to improve the world, word by word.

BARBARA CORCORAN

Businesswoman

March 10, 1949

Dyslexia

Businesswoman Barbara Corcoran didn't think she'd be successful. She had a hard time in school, just passing with D's in most classes. Her classmates and teachers didn't think much of her, and in turn, Barbara didn't think much of herself. Growing up in the fifties, Barbara was told that only smart people became successful. Smart people got all the good things in life, and everyone else was destined for a lifetime of hard, unrewarding work. Barbara had been told that she wasn't smart, so she didn't believe she was capable of being successful. But it turned out, Barbara was wrong about that—and everyone else was, too.

As an adult, Barbara found success in real estate. Real estate involves the buying and selling of property—which includes land, buildings, and homes. She became one of the most successful real estate agents in the United States and also taught other people how to become successful. Barbara credits her success to something that held her back and inspired her to prove everyone wrong: dyslexia.

Motivation

Barbara grew up in a large family of ten children. As the second oldest child, she had a sense of responsibility early on. She watched as her father jumped from job to job and treated her mother poorly. In second grade, a teacher called her a horrible name because she had trouble reading. The interaction embarrassed Barbara and caused her to feel insecure throughout her childhood, and even into adulthood. It wasn't just the teacher who bullied her. Her peers also began to call her names and tease her about reading slow. But this bullying motivated Barbara to prove everyone wrong. She worked hard to learn how to read better and gain the skills she needed to pass her classes. Despite all this hard work, Barbara still didn't make the honor roll. In fact, she barely passed her classes. Still, she went to college and did well enough to graduate.

Barbara was restless. By the time she was twenty-three she had worked about twenty jobs. She just couldn't find a career that fit her personality. Unlike some of her peers, Barbara had not found the perfect job right out school. She didn't have a plan. She remembered how she felt in school and began to doubt herself. Barbara decided that maybe being her own boss was the way to go, and she founded a real estate company in the 1970s. But selling real estate was also a challenge. She had to quickly adapt to a fast-paced sales environment. Barbara had to learn how to sell homes in a way that set her apart. That meant she'd have to think outside the box, something she'd been used to doing her whole life. She found ways to make her properties stand out, either by adding more detailed descriptions, or being one of the first realtors to list homes on the internet. It would take years before Barbara got the hang of it, but she knew that slow and steady progress would help her win the race.

Barbara's career in real estate had many ups and downs, but she never let the failures bother her. Instead, she saw them as opportunities to bounce back. Barbara has said, "To be successful, you have to be good at getting back up. I see failure as a big bouncing ball. The harder you hit a ball on the concrete, the bigger the bounce coming back up."

In 2001, after almost thirty years of hard work, she had her biggest bounce back yet when she sold her business for over $60 million! Barbara realized her success didn't happen by chance. The name calling and bullying in her youth had motivated her to prove everyone wrong.

As an adult, Barbara discovered something important that changed her perspective on the challenges she faced with learning. When her son was in elementary school, he was diagnosed with dyslexia, and Barbara realized she had it, too. Once the diagnosis was confirmed, Barbara felt some relief—and gratitude. She had spent years feeling insecure about her intelligence when in fact, she just learned things differently. Barbara still felt the sting of her teachers' harsh words and her classmates' cruel jokes, but those early experiences had also prepared her for the tough business world. They helped her develop empathy for others because it was not given to her when she needed it. Most of all, they helped her adopt a no-nonsense attitude that was necessary to build her own multimillion-dollar business.

The Common Denominator

Barbara didn't stop once she sold her real estate business. She used the money she made to invest in other people's businesses, and she mentored other entrepreneurs, people who want to start their own businesses like she did. Her next big break came when she joined the popular TV show *Shark Tank*. On the show, she and five other judges listen to contestants pitch their business ideas. The contestants compete for the judges to invest in their business. The show has created many successful businesses, giving opportunities to people who may not have succeeded otherwise.

While working with the other judges, Barbara noticed that they all had more in common than just being successful business owners. She found that many of her colleagues faced the same learning challenges she did. Three of the six *Shark Tank* judges have dyslexia: Barbara, Kevin O'Leary, and Daymond John. Barbara shared a theory that dyslexia may be an asset to business owners. She saw dyslexia as a strength in her own life and noticed that it had also served as a great strength in helping many of the savvy businesspeople she knew to see the world differently and think outside of the box.

Old Habits

Although Barbara has fans around the world and has proven herself as a capable businesswoman, she still has bouts of insecurity. She said, "I feel like my whole life I've been insecure about looking not smart. So I feel like everything I do is a constant attempt to prove to whoever's around me that I can measure up." Many neurodiverse people can relate.

With over fifty years of experience in business management, investing, and real estate, Barbara has made a name for herself in a male-dominated industry. As one of the few women featured on *Shark Tank*, Barbara has gained a fan base because of her quick wit, empathy, and ability to understand business needs. She's a risk-taker, gathering information and making smart decisions to help new businesses grow. Barbara is proof that success is not always about how you start, but has a lot to do with how you finish.

ATOOSA RUBENSTEIN

Magazine Editor

January 13, 1972

Dyslexia

At age twenty-six, Atoosa Rubenstein was at the top of the world. She had founded *CosmoGirl!*, a teen magazine spin-off of the popular *Cosmopolitan* magazine, and was the youngest editor in chief in her company's history. Just a few years later, she was promoted to another popular magazine, *Seventeen*. During the height of her career, she even created and produced a reality TV show on MTV. This was the age of teen magazines. Teen pop stars like Justin Timberlake and Britney Spears appeared on the covers. The magazines covered topics ranging from top lip gloss colors to tips to help you get ready for prom.

There were tons of teen magazines to choose from, each promising something different or appealing to a certain crowd. But Atoosa's magazines were special. She was known for answering fan mail, and her editor letters, letters to her readers, were unusually honest and vulnerable. She'd share her old, awkward childhood photos and reassure readers that it was normal not to look like the models in the magazines. They didn't have to compare themselves to superstars. And beauty was not the key to happiness. It was a message that many teens needed to hear. One time she even shared her struggle with excessive body hair—a subject many teens had issues with or were ashamed of. She connected with her audience in a way no one had done before.

Atoosa hoped to share positivity and encourage teens to love themselves, giving advice she wished she'd had during her own teenage years—and she readily admitted those years were difficult for her. One headline labeled her a "Former High School Loser," which was a tacky and cruel way to showcase her struggles in high school. As a teen she was bullied for lots of things. On any regular day someone would pick on her because she was an Iranian immigrant, or maybe they just didn't like her looks. Other days it was her bushy eyebrows, her lisp, or her dyslexia. Dyslexia is a learning difference that affects reading. A person with dyslexia may have trouble with reading comprehension, spelling, or reading aloud. Words were a bit of a problem for Atoosa. Although Atoosa grew up to become America's "big sister," she still had to manage dyslexia in an industry where every word mattered.

Humble Beginnings

Atoosa Behnegar was born in Tehran, Iran, on January 13, 1972. Her father was a colonel in the Iranian Air Force before relocating to New York. The Behnegar family didn't speak English when they moved to America and didn't know anyone. Mr. Behnegar worked as a cab driver and money was tight. Adjusting to America was difficult for Atoosa. She was different, and at that time different wasn't seen as good. Her lisp and dyslexia made her stand out. But she found comfort in teen magazines. The magazines helped her understand American culture and what her peers were interested in. Atoosa looked through magazines for answers to everything. Even when she went to college, she'd keep a magazine under her books. By that time, Atoosa knew she wanted to work in the magazine industry.

She started as an assistant at *Cosmopolitan* magazine. There, Atoosa noticed something interesting: instead of people making fun of her looks, they complimented them! From strangers to coworkers, people began to comment on how beautiful Atoosa was. She may not have fit in growing up, but now she had found a place where she was popular. Atoosa didn't let popularity get to her head. She did what she had always done, even when she wasn't popular—be nice to everyone. She offered to help everyone and treated everyone with kindness. Soon, her hard work and positive attitude paid off.

Her company was looking for an editor for a teen version of *Cosmopolitan* and asked Atoosa to create a mock issue, or a sample of what it should look like. Atoosa was excited. She did such a good job that they made her editor in chief of the new magazine, *CosmoGIRL!*. She was only twenty-six, the youngest editor in chief at any magazine in her company's history. In this role, she wanted to be more than a pretty face. Atoosa knew what it was like to be bullied or feel out of place. She knew that being cool or popular shouldn't be based on looks or how well a person read. She wanted to tell teenagers that they were smart, capable, and beautiful just the way they were.

Coming up with good ideas was no problem, but as an editor, she'd have to read, write, and approve what stories went into the magazine. And processing tons of reading was a challenge for her. She had to make it work. She had learned to manage her dyslexia as a child, but reading so much for her job was different. Now everything she wrote would be read by thousands of people. Was she up for the challenge?

The Right Words

Atoosa faced her challenges head-on. She got assistance to help her process all the reading she had to do. She took her time. Sometimes she had memos read aloud, which helped her comprehend the meaning better. Having dyslexia also meant that Atoosa made every word count. She encouraged her team to write simple, zippy headlines that were easy to process for her and for readers. She made sure the pages of the magazine were designed with fun, inviting visual elements, not just long blocks of text. Dyslexia didn't go away, but as she got older, Atoosa learned different strategies to conquer it.

And along the way, she became the voice of comfort for teens across America. As editor in chief, she won over thousands of hearts by speaking to her readers with kindness and encouragement. Atoosa felt that teenagers dealt with a lot of pressures—something she knew all too well. Growing up, magazines had guided Atoosa through her teenage years. As a grown-up, she helped her readers do the same. She became the voice that told them that everything would be all right, that their feelings were valid; they were not alone.

SELENA GOMEZ

Actress and Singer

July 22, 1992

Bipolar Disorder

Selena Gomez was a child star who blossomed into a multitalented actress, singer, and businesswoman. By the time she was twenty, Selena had charmed legions of fans and garnered numerous accolades for her supporting role in the TV show *Hannah Montana* with actress Miley Cyrus and her lead role as Alex Russo in *Wizards of Waverly Place*. She was a teen idol seemingly on top of the entertainment world. However, Selena had faced health challenges that threatened her flourishing career. She openly shared her struggles with depression and anxiety. But behind the scenes, the young star worried something else was not right. She often felt exhausted and unhappy. Selena went through periods when she was extremely happy and energetic, and just as quickly she'd feel extremely sad and emotionally drained. She continued to work, even putting out music and promoting it with cross-country tours. Selena kept busy, but she wondered why she felt so up and down—was it more than depression and anxiety?

Selena spent time with therapists and in treatment centers to help her feel better and more like herself. All the while, her status as a superstar continued to grow. Soon, her social media following swelled to over one hundred million!

Although Selena appreciated the love from her fans, she also felt overwhelmed by the number of people who had opinions on everything from her looks to her career. Some of the comments she saw were negative and hurtful. The noise, the negativity, the hectic schedule, and the heavy workload took their toll. Selena soon began taking breaks from social media. But the up-and-down feelings persisted. In 2018, Selena went to a treatment center for help and was diagnosed with bipolar disorder.

Bipolar disorder is a condition that causes someone's mood, concentration, or activity to drastically change. People with bipolar disorder may experience sharp, sudden swings between periods of extreme positivity and periods of deep sadness. The condition can affect the way someone processes information and make it difficult to complete tasks. For Selena, bipolar disorder made it difficult to manage the highs and lows of fame. In 2020, during a live stream, Selena revealed her diagnosis to fans. She shared that when she was finally diagnosed, she wanted to learn everything she could about bipolar disorder. Having more information helped dispel Selena's fears and reassured her that she could successfully manage her condition.

Learning about her disorder wasn't the first time Selena faced challenges. She had to face her fears at an early age and understand the power of persistence.

Perseverance

As a child, Selena was exposed to the entertainment world early on. At ten years old, she began acting on a popular children's show called *Barney & Friends*. The experience would help shape Selena into an actress, teaching her how to work on a television set and become more comfortable on the stage. Selena appeared in several episodes before moving on to other television shows.

While Selena was booking more and more roles, her mother, Mandy, worked multiple jobs and supported Selena's big-screen dreams. Mandy was a young single mother who knew her daughter would be a star. Sometimes Mandy and Selena had to scrape together money just to put gas in their car to get to auditions. Still, Mandy made sure that Selena got to auditions and was able to showcase her talent. She taught Selena to be strong and to persevere through hard times.

By the time Selena was fifteen, she was a regular on *Hannah Montana*. Soon after, she landed the lead role on Disney's *Wizards of Waverly Place*. She would go on to become one of the highest-paid child stars of all time! As she continued acting, she embarked on a singing career as well, starting with hits like "Tell Me Something I Don't Know" and "Love You Like a Love Song." She and her mom were stable, and it seemed that perseverance had paid off. From television to movie appearances to music and magazine covers, Selena Gomez was on a winning streak. However, as she moved into her early twenties, she was struggling with both her mental and physical health. She felt immense pressure not to let her fans down, but she didn't want to let herself down, either.

In 2017, Selena was noticeably quiet. She'd taken a break from social media and her career over the course of the summer. Fans were concerned. In September, Selena revealed that she'd had a kidney transplant due to lupus. Lupus is a disease that causes the immune system to attack its own organs, leading to inflammation throughout the body. It can be a painful condition, affecting one's skin, muscles, lungs, and kidneys. Anxiety and depression, like Selena experienced, can also be side effects of lupus. Fortunately, Selena recovered well from her organ transplant, but she would still have to manage her illness and its side effects. Selena told her fans, "I need to face this head-on to ensure I am doing everything possible to be my best. I know I am not alone by sharing this; I hope others will be encouraged to address their own issues."

Mental Health Advocate

Since revealing her bipolar diagnosis, Selena has worked hard to manage her well-being. She has also kept working, releasing more music, appearing in more hit television shows, and launching a popular beauty brand, Rare Beauty. She's also made history becoming the most-nominated Latina producer in television.

Selena even produced a documentary about her life with bipolar disorder and started a fundraising organization to help other people better manage their mental illness. She has become a respected advocate for mental health—speaking frequently about how important it is to pay attention to how we feel, think, and act with ourselves and others.

Selena remains beloved for her talents and for the honesty and vulnerability she's shown throughout her career. By opening up about her experiences with anxiety, depression, lupus, and bipolar disorder, she arms her fans with information, dispels fears about these conditions, and inspires others to prioritize their own health, too.

DAVID BECKHAM

Soccer Player

May 2, 1975

Obsessive-Compulsive Disorder

In May 2013, David Beckham suited up for the big game as he'd done for over a decade. He had created a long and successful career as one of the most famous soccer players in the world. He'd played—and won—in various countries and even sponsored a team in the United States. David Beckham helped popularize soccer in the United States, where (American) football reigned. He had rocketed from soccer star to global celebrity, complete with television appearances, lucrative endorsement deals, modeling opportunities as a trendsetting style icon, and even a movie named after him—*Bend It Like Beckham*. As his fame grew, so did the popularity of soccer. However, at age thirty-eight, David knew it was time to hang up his cleats. Soccer was a physical sport and he'd been playing it at a high level since he was around ten years old. His body had been banged up through years of kicking, jumping, and falling down.

As the game came to a close, David cried, overcome with emotion. His teammates cheered him on as he walked off the field. The fans chanted his name, flooding the stadium with adoration. David was soccer's hero and soccer was David's calling. For many fans, David Beckham was as close to the perfect athlete as one could get. He was charming, skilled, smart, and hardworking. However, very few people knew just how hard David worked to keep up a perfect persona. He lived a very strict life where order and organization were his top priorities. He lined up drinks in his refrigerator, ensuring they were uniform in color or brand. He even put everything into straight lines or pairs—no odd numbers! David had a strict bedtime routine that included thorough cleaning to ensure his kitchen was spotless each night. He could not help but organize things around him. Being clean and orderly is generally a positive thing, but David's obsession was something else.

In 2023, David opened up about having obsessive-compulsive disorder. Obsessive-compulsive disorder, often shortened to OCD, causes someone to have recurring thoughts or obsessions that drive them to repetitive actions. People with this disorder can't help but perform the actions they keep thinking about. For some, they may have to wash their hands a certain number of times to feel satisfied. For others, they may need an exceptionally clean environment or for all their shirts to be one color. These repetitive actions can be tied to negative thoughts, too. People with OCD may experience feelings like worry, distress, or fear that something bad may happen if they change their strict routine. David described living with OCD as "tiring," but it is something he had been living with since he began playing soccer as a child.

Becoming Beckham

From an early age, David Beckham learned the sport of soccer by watching his family's favorite team, Manchester United, on television. David grew up in London, England, and spent most of his time playing soccer—or football as it is called there and in most countries outside the United States. He was a youth phenomenon, gaining the attention of coaches across England. It seemed that soccer came easily to him, and he dreamed of playing for the Manchester United when he grew up. By the time he was eleven, Manchester United officials had already spotted his talent. They asked David to try out for their youth league, a program the team sponsored for promising young players. David was thrilled, and his family was proud.

David was not only talented; he took the sport very seriously, playing with precision unusual for someone so young. Although David was a skilled player, he did have one disadvantage: he was smaller than many of the other boys. That only fueled him to work harder and prove himself. His coaches noticed that he always stayed after practice to improve his kicks. It became a routine for him. Consistency—whether that be sticking to the same structure at practice or the repetition of perfecting a skill on the field—is a great attribute for an athlete. But off the field, David's seriousness, precision, and preference for routines could sometimes make life difficult. He preferred a tidy, organized environment—something that was quite different from other kids his age. And his family noticed that David could be prickly when faced with disorder or interruptions to his routines. But his family supported his rigid schedules and began to understand that to David, sticking to a routine was the key to winning.

By eighteen, David was a professional athlete for Manchester United—the soccer club he had dreamed of joining. It wasn't long before David began dominating the soccer field. By the time he was twenty-two, he was a household name in England. His game-winning plays entered the list of great sports moments. His "bending" free kicks—when one gives the ball a spin to make it curve while flying through the air—are legendary to this day. Although David was a great player and teammate, he still faced challenges in his career. Journalists often criticized him for playing too rough. In 1998, David was thrown out of an important World Cup game for kicking an opponent. The media and many fans blamed David for the loss. Around the same time, David was becoming a bigger and bigger celebrity, so when he struggled on the field, critics often suggested that his fame or his personal life were affecting his game. Still, David stuck to his routine and played as hard as he could. Throughout his career, he played in England, Spain, Italy, France, and the United States. He even won league titles in four different countries. David had conquered soccer and it was time to hang up his cleats. Things were changing for the megapopular athlete, and with those changes came new challenges.

After Soccer

Over a decade after retiring, David is revered as one of the best athletes in the world. He is known for his perseverance and dedication to the sport. However, David has also worked to make a name for himself outside of sports. He gives to charities and has made it a point to bring awareness to obsessive-compulsive disorder by opening up about the challenges he has faced while managing his disorder.

In his 2023 documentary, *Beckham*, David talks about how tiring his routine is. He explains how he prepares his clothes a week in advance and how his disorder compels him to clean up excessively. Although he scored many goals in soccer, the stress of managing his OCD was something he could not easily win. However, by talking openly about his challenges and how he manages day-to-day, David has created more acceptance for those who have OCD. While there may never be another soccer player who can bend the ball quite like him, there are countless athletes and fans who are inspired by his willingness to conquer OCD one goal at a time.

PHARRELL WILLIAMS

Music Producer, Singer, and Creative Director

April 5, 1973

Synesthesia

In 2023, Pharrell Williams became the creative director for luxury fashion brand Louis Vuitton. Pharrell already had a hugely successful career as a music producer and songwriter. Now, he'd be designing clothes and establishing a creative vision for one of the most popular brands in the world. Although Pharrell being hired surprised some people in the fashion industry, he had always had a knack for style. He'd been turning heads on red carpets for years, and was once named the world's most stylish man by a popular men's magazine. He'd even worked in fashion before, launching his own clothing brand called Billionaire Boys Club, and collaborating with Adidas and Chanel, another luxury brand. But Pharrell would have big shoes to fill. He was taking over for Virgil Abloh, the first Black creative director for Louis Vuitton. Abloh had passed away unexpectedly just a few years before. Fashion fans wondered how Pharrell would measure up to such an iconic designer.

Pharrell had proven he could make hits and set trends in the music industry. But many people had no idea that his catchy, futuristic beats were a product of his sensory-sensitive mind. Pharrell is a synesthete. Synesthetes, people who have synesthesia, process sensory information differently than most people do. For Pharrell, sounds are visual and appear in many colors. Visualizing sounds helped Pharrell make iconic songs and signature beats. Now, he was turning his uncanny mind to a new creative challenge. With over thirty years' experience creating bold, visionary work, Pharrell was set to make his mark in fashion as a trendsetter and hitmaker.

Futuristic

When he was young, Pharrell experimented with making beats with whatever he could find around his house. He'd use whisks, pots, and kitchen appliances to create sounds. His family encouraged him to take up an instrument and join the school band. In middle school, he went to band camp and learned more about combining instruments and creating music. Pharrell met a fellow band kid, Chad, during seventh grade and they became fast friends. Chad and Pharrell began making music together, crafting unique beats and writing song lyrics. They formed a group, The Neptunes, and while still in high school, they were discovered by a major producer. By 1996, just a few years after high school, The Neptunes had made a name for themselves as songwriters and producers. They became so popular that everyone wanted to work with them, from hip-hop stars like Jay-Z to pop artists like Britney Spears; the Neptunes' sound—which combined punchy drum beats, soul, and rock music with pop—captivated airwaves and televisions around the world.

The Neptunes' sound dominated the early twenty-first century, but Pharrell's unique fashion sense also attracted attention. His personal style was influenced by skateboard culture—wearing baggy pants, trucker caps, and sneakers. Eventually, his style evolved, and giant, sometimes brightly colored hats became his signature accessory, along with futuristic, geometrically shaped glasses. In 2003, he created his own fashion line and soon after began partnering with other brands to design everything from eyewear and sneakers to jewelry.

Pharrell's hitmaking continued as he ventured into film. He wrote several songs for the *Despicable Me* franchise, including the hit "Happy," which won a Grammy and numerous other awards. He voiced the narrator in an animated version of Dr. Seuss's *The Grinch*. Pharrell's success was off the charts.

Seeing Sounds

While his talent is the major reason for his rise to the top, he credits his synesthesia as another reason for his uncanny creative ability. He even describes producing music as putting his "colors" on it.

Pharrell has described his learning process as "different." When he was a kid, his mind would start wandering whenever it was time to read. He had to force himself to focus and often forgot the information he read. He also realized early on that "seeing" sounds wasn't something everyone could do. Fortunately, he's always embraced his differences as pathways to help him become a stronger creative. He even named his third album *Seeing Sounds*, a nod to his super-processing ability. He says, "It's the only way that I can identify what something sounds like. I know when something is in key because it either matches the same color or it doesn't. Or it feels different and it doesn't feel right." Synesthesia is central to Pharrell's music making.

Pop Culture Phenom

Just a few months after Pharrell joined Louis Vuitton, it was time for his first fashion show. Would he uphold the traditions of the storied fashion brand or embrace his own unique style? Could he do both? Could the iconic music producer fit into the fashion world? On June 20, 2023, he debuted his first collection to Fashion Week attendees in Paris and live streamed the event to viewers around the world. In true Pharrell fashion, he combined the traditional print of the brand's logo with vibrant colors and bold designs. Many of his models showcased tailored short sets, a look he had popularized on red carpets. He even included geometric glasses, a nod to his signature eyewear. Overall, the fashion journalists loved what they saw. And so did those watching at home, prompting a social media frenzy over the hot new styles Pharrell had created. Once again, Pharrell was making hits and setting trends. In 2024, Pharell's colorful life story was made into a LEGO movie called *Piece by Piece*, an ode to his ability to build incredible things from his imagination. His vision, which includes his unique way of processing sounds, continues to inspire the next generation of neurodivergent creatives and encourages us all to chart our own paths to the top.

MILES CHAMLEY-WATSON

Fencer

December 3, 1989

Attention Deficit Hyperactivity Disorder

The sport of fencing is strictly rooted in tradition. The competition is straightforward—two fencers face each other on a long mat, they lunge, and the point is given to the person whose blunted sword touches the other fencer first. The sport is fast and extremely precise. Traditionally, there are no extreme moves or tricks. Fortunately, tradition is always one step away from innovation. Miles Chamley-Watson was just that innovation.

In 2013, Miles became the first American male to win the individual World Fencing Championship title. But it had taken years of innovating before Miles reached the top of his sport. At his first world championship, four years earlier, Miles, standing at six foot four, had done something unexpected: he whipped his sword around the back of his head to score a point on his opponent's chest. The difficult move was quick and precise. The crowd was in awe—no one had ever done a move like that in a fencing match. The referee had to stop the match to review the move. Once he confirmed that the action was legal, it went viral! People across the world watched Miles's cool move and dubbed it "the Chamley-Watson." Armed with his signature move and a new fan base, Miles would continue to innovate his way into the top ranks of the sport.

Miles broke tradition in fencing off the strip, too. After his move went viral, popular brands hired him to sponsor their products. He channeled his love of fashion into modeling gigs and high profile fashion shoots for magazines like *Vogue*. He walked the runway at Fashion Weeks, attended the exclusive Met Gala, and partnered with companies like Nike. He is one of the most followed fencers on social media, solidifying his status as an influencer. For fencers, corporate sponsorships and celebrity status were unheard of. But Miles had been an outsider from the moment he entered the sport. He came from humble beginnings without the upper-class background common to many competitive fencers. As a six-foot-four Black man with tattoo art, Miles was a unique sight in the fencing world, which is predominantly white and wealthy. Also, he has attention deficit hyperactivity disorder (ADHD), a diagnosis that has set him apart from most of his fellow competitors. From an early age, Miles had learned that doing things his own way would take him further than he could imagine.

The American Dream

Miles moved to the United States with his mom and stepdad when he was just nine years old. The trip across the ocean from the United Kingdom was long, and Miles didn't know what to expect. Unfortunately, he had a hard time fitting in with American classmates. They made fun of his accent and made him feel like an outsider. On top of that, Miles had a hard time focusing and often let his anger get the best of him. He quickly became known as a hothead.

Fortunately, things turned around for Miles when his parents enrolled him in a program for kids with ADHD. There, he got more attention and learned skills to manage his feelings, behavior, and focus. One teacher encouraged him to try out fencing as she suspected the sport's strict rules and calm environment would help him. Miles was reluctant; fencing didn't seem as cool as the soccer games he watched growing up. He tried it anyway, and kids made fun of him. Miles just couldn't catch a break! But the teasing had a surprising consequence: "I always had the motivation to prove people wrong," he said. Soon Miles began to love the sport and chose his special weapon—foil.

Fencing has three weapons to choose from: foil, saber, and épée. For Miles, the flexibility and light weight of the foil made it the best choice. A foilist scores a point by hitting their opponent first in a small, targeted area on the chest or arm. It's a game of super speed and precision. Fencing is a one-on-one sport that requires concentration and thinking ahead, considering your opponent's next move. It's like chess and sword fighting! For people with ADHD, fencing can help with focus, and it appeals to those who need to constantly move. With fencing, Miles had found his rhythm in the bustling city of New York. He began to compete at youth events and across the nation. He even competed against people from across the world. He has participated in three Olympic Games, even earning a bronze medal in the team event in 2016.

As Miles's star power rose, people outside the sport took notice. Soon, Miles began modeling for top brands. His vibrant personality, energy, and tall frame kept him busy with fashion and luxury brand sponsorships. Miles stood out—and because of that, he gained more and more recognition. He realized that people loved his unique personality and style, and that his ADHD diagnosis would not hinder him. Miles was able to achieve a career in modeling and professional fencing—by being himself.

Innovator

An Olympian with over fifteen first-place wins under his belt, Miles has made fencing more widespread while he has become one of the most popular fencers in the world. Miles shows that success can come to those who are comfortable being themselves. As a kid, Miles struggled with his ADHD and often got frustrated. Fortunately, he used fencing as an outlet for his strong emotions. The sport helped him to better use his energy and learn how to focus.

Miles Chamley-Watson is one of the most innovative competitors in the sport of fencing, creating unique moves at the speed of light. Although his speed and athleticism sometimes seems superhuman, Miles has overcome some of the same circumstances as everyone else—being bullied, feeling like an outsider, and worrying that what makes you different isn't special at all. But by doing things his way, adding his unique flair, Miles was able to break through in a sport that was often not inclusive. He brought excitement and fresh eyes to fencing and attracted diverse fans who favored flair and innovation while still paying homage to the sport's regal tradition. He said, "I always want to be remembered as someone who was never afraid to take a risk." Miles understood that he'd have to take risks and trust his instincts to make sports history.

JAMIE GRACE HARPER

Musician

November 25, 1991

Tourette's Syndrome

On February 12, 2012, singer and songwriter Jamie Grace attended the 54th Annual Grammy ceremony. At age twenty, she was the year's youngest nominee, honored in the category Best Contemporary Christian Music Song for "Hold Me," her duet with singer TobyMac. Jamie had been singing and writing music since she was a teenager. She loved Southern gospel and country music and created a sound infused with both of her favorite genres. When her song exploded on the charts, Jamie Grace became a popular star in faith-based music almost overnight.

As she walked down the red carpet at the Grammys, she was amazed at the people vying for her attention and gave interviews for major outlets. The Grammys are the biggest awards in music. Being Grammy-nominated is a dream come true for most artists, the ultimate recognition from music-industry experts. Jamie was appreciative of the opportunity and couldn't wait to hear the results. Although she didn't win a Grammy Award, she knew being nominated was a testament to her hard work and faith. And just ten days after the Grammy Award ceremony, Jamie Grace was nominated for four Dove Awards, given by the

Gospel Music Association. Two months later, she won a Dove Award for New Artist of the Year!

The nominations and wins were proof that her talent was bigger than any challenges she may have faced. And for Jamie, the challenges were plenty. The young musician was openly neurodivergent, with a diagnosis of Tourette's syndrome. Her experience managing her diagnosis made her resilient in facing the highs and lows of both her music career and health. And over time, Jamie used that resilience to help her write music that deeply resonated with other people who faced their own challenges.

Honesty and Positivity

Jamie grew up singing and playing instruments in her parents' church. Music helped Jamie express her feelings and hone her budding talent. She played the guitar and would eventually learn to play the drums and piano. While music brought her comfort, by age eleven, Jamie began having tics, which became more aggressive and unpredictable. Her legs would flail, kicking anyone around her. Her neck would dangerously jerk and sometimes cause her to hit her head on nearby objects. Her parents were concerned. They didn't want her to hurt herself or someone else. At age eleven, she was diagnosed with Tourette's syndrome along with an anxiety disorder and ADHD. These diagnoses were daunting, but Jamie and her family knew that together they could manage her needs.

Jamie's Tourette's also involved echolalia. Echolalia is a type of stimming where someone may repeat words or phrases they hear. It's like having a short quote or song stuck in your head, but instead of repeating or singing the song in your head, echolalia causes you to verbalize it either right after you hear it or at random points throughout the day.

Dealing with the effects of Tourette's and ADHD was difficult for Jamie. Her severe symptoms continued well into her teen years. Jamie's body was growing and her random movements would sometimes cause a lot of embarrassment in public, like when she knocked something over while shopping in a store. Being a teenager is tough, but it was especially challenging for Jamie when she felt she was losing control of her body. Jamie also had to manage an anxiety disorder. Anxiety can cause extreme feelings of worry or fear. These feelings can interfere with daily activities. For Jamie, anxiety caused her to overthink decisions and worry about how others perceived her. She experienced a lot of fear and frustration. Jamie turned to her faith and music to help cope with her strong feelings and restlessness. She began creating videos on YouTube to share her experiences. She answered questions, gave advice, and showed the world what it was really like to be a teenager with Tourette's syndrome. Viewers loved her honesty and positivity. This gave Jamie the confidence to start posting cover songs and original music to YouTube; and viewers loved these videos, too! Before long, music producers saw Jamie's videos and helped her start recording songs professionally.

Marching On

As an adult, Jamie still experiences tics and echolalia, but she has lots of tools and routines to help her manage her diagnosis. She prioritizes quiet time and self-care to keep stress from exacerbating her symptoms. She ensures that she is safe while experiencing tics, to avoid physically harming herself or people around her. She tries distracting herself, which can help alleviate her tics. Above all, she has discovered that moving, dancing, and singing can keep her calm.

And she continues to share her music and her personal experiences on YouTube. In 2020, Jamie released a new song, "Marching On." It was inspired by her diagnoses and, when making the song, Jamie did something unique: she recorded her tics and incorporated them in the music. Recording her tics was a special experience for Jamie. She said, "Some people with Tourette's have explained it like a sneeze. You can hold it in as much as you'd like, but eventually it's going to show back up . . . So pressing 'record' and letting those walls fall down felt like pure freedom."

By creating music from her tics, Jamie is continuing to spread a positive message about Tourette's syndrome and about persisting no matter what challenges you may face. She explained, "The things that you might use to tear me down or the things that you might think will hold me back are literally . . . the foundation for my soundtrack of my life. And that is the anthem of my life, finding the positivity even in Tourette's syndrome."

Normal

Jamie's online presence continues to bring awareness to Tourette's syndrome while showcasing her unique personality and talent. Her YouTube videos both inspire and educate those interested in music or learning more about loving yourself for who you are. And in addition to making her own music, Jamie now mentors the next generation of young gospel, pop, and contemporary Christian musicians, too. Jamie credits her faith for helping her to accept the things that make her different, saying, "It was God who knew all along that Tourette's syndrome—the thing I was most ashamed of—was really my greatest source of strength. He didn't make my tics go away. He knew my songs would resonate because Tourette's made me dig deep."

TONY SNELL

Basketball Player

November 10, 1991

Autism

When Tony Snell and his wife took their son, Karter, to the doctor, they were concerned about his development. By eighteen months, toddlers are expected to say three or more words, play pretend, and point to things that interest them. But Karter was not reaching these milestones. He hadn't begun talking and was stimming. He hoarded toys but didn't really play with them. While many kids develop at different rates, developmental delays can sometimes suggest neurodiversity. In Karter's case, the doctor wanted to test Karter by having a specialist observe his communication, social interaction, play, and behavior. The doctor suspected Karter might have autism spectrum disorder.

Autism spectrum disorder was new to Tony. He wasn't sure what the disorder was, so he did some research to make sure he knew how to help his son. Tony had experience watching basketball tapes and studying plays as a professional athlete—all in an effort to defeat his opponents. But now, to understand what his son was facing, he'd have to follow a different playbook.

Tony learned that folks on the autism spectrum sometimes have trouble connecting to others. He learned that autism could affect the way someone processes information or the way they communicate. He read about symptoms of autism—like stimming, avoiding eye contact, and social avoidance. Tony recognized these symptoms all too well. He'd had some of these same challenges himself. When Karter's results came back and confirmed that he had autism, Tony knew that he needed to get tested, too. At thirty-one, Tony was diagnosed with autism.

Tony was relieved. Now he had an explanation for why he'd felt different growing up. However, Tony wondered how doctors missed his diagnosis for years. He wondered what his life would have been like if he'd been diagnosed as early as his son had. Tony wasn't sure about the past, but he was certain about his future. He knew that his diagnosis wouldn't just help himself and his son. He wanted to help other people who felt different and just couldn't put their finger on why. Tony explained, "I just want to change lives and inspire people" by showing that neurodivergent people can achieve greatness.

Focused on Big Dreams

Tony Snell grew up in the Watts neighborhood of Los Angeles. The neighborhood dealt with crime and gang violence, but Tony—tall, shy, and independent—always stayed out of trouble. He felt disconnected from people his age, so he often stuck to himself and focused on basketball. Eventually, Tony moved to Arizona and finished high school there.

Tony was recruited to play college basketball at the University of Nevada, Las Vegas, where he excelled on the court but remained shy. He dreamed of playing professional basketball for the NBA, a dream that wouldn't be easy to achieve. Tony had the talent and the height, but he needed the opportunity. He worked hard and practiced, and impressively, Tony entered the NBA at just twenty-one years old. He went on to play for the Chicago Bulls, Milwaukee

Bucks, Detroit Pistons, Atlanta Hawks, Portland Trail Blazers, and the New Orleans Pelicans. In 2021, he became the first and only player in NBA history to record a 50-50-100 season, showing exceptional scoring accuracy on field goals (making 51.5 percent of his shots), three-pointers (56.9 percent), and free throws (100 percent). Traveling across the nation as an NBA player kept Tony busy, but following social expectations didn't feel quite right. He met different people and spent a lot of time with his teammates, but he didn't feel connected to his peers and didn't know why.

You Want to Know . . .

Why are neurodivergent people different?
We don't know why some people process things differently than others. However, neurodivergent brains process, learn, and behave differently than neurotypical—or what is considered normal—brains.

Achieving Greatness

In 2022, Tony left the NBA, and the following year, he joined a minor league basketball team. He also began to spend more time at home with his family. Around that time, Tony and his son were both diagnosed with autism. He explained that his diagnosis "just made my whole life, everything about my life, make so much sense. It was like . . . putting some 3-D glasses on."

By sharing his story, Tony has brought attention to the lack of early diagnoses in underserved communities. According to CDC data, in the past, children of color were less likely to be diagnosed with autism than white children. Many people lack the knowledge or resources to seek out an early diagnosis and others may be afraid to label their kids early on. But early diagnosis is one of the most powerful tools available to support and treat autistic children. The earlier that children get help with speech, processing, and occupational therapy, the more successful they can become. The good news is, according to a 2023 CDC report, that autism diagnoses are on the rise. This means that more children can get the help they need to thrive—just like Tony's son.

Tony hopes to be a role model for others who have an autism diagnosis, and for parents of children with autism. He and his family started a foundation to promote autism acceptance and education. The foundation focuses on supporting underserved communities. "It's taboo in the Black community to talk about your disability," Tony stated. "I want to normalize the concept that everyone's brain is wired differently." He is also motivated by his family. "I want to make sure my son knows that I have his back," Tony said. "When I was a kid, I felt different . . . but now I could show him that I'm right here with you, [and] we're going to ride this thing together. We're going to grow together, and we're going to accomplish a lot of things together."

While Tony achieved greatness on the court, his work outside of the court is just as significant. By promoting autism acceptance, he champions those who are different and encourages them to be more comfortable in their own skin—by following their own playbook. Tony is leading the charge and sending a powerful message of acceptance not just for his own kids, but also for countless others on the autism spectrum.

DANIEL RADCLIFFE

Actor

July 23, 1989

Dyspraxia

Daniel Radcliffe grew up acting as one of the most popular fictional characters in the world, Harry Potter. He was just ten when he began acting professionally. He had been having a hard time in school, and his parents thought that going to an acting audition might be a fun, unique experience to lift his spirits. They were all surprised when he got the part! It was an even bigger surprise when he was cast as Harry Potter, the lead role in the movie adaptation of a bestselling book series, soon after.

Playing the popular character didn't spell the end of his troubles, though. At school Daniel had admittedly never been a great student, and keeping up with a hectic filming schedule further affected his grades. He already had a great paying job as an actor, so studying wasn't a priority for him. On top of that, some of his classmates bullied him. As his schedule got more demanding, he spent less and less time in school. He much preferred being on the film set, where he felt like he belonged. And while filming, he got individual tutoring, which better suited his unique learning needs.

Daniel starred in eight Harry Potter films, and fans all over the world loved his portrayal of the boy wizard. The series broke box office records and became one of the highest-grossing movie franchises in history.

About a week after the final movie in the series, *Harry Potter and the Deathly Hallows: Part 2*, was released, Daniel turned twenty-two. More than a decade had passed since he first auditioned to play Harry Potter. Acting in the films had changed Daniel's life, but it had also consumed his life. He didn't want to be "the boy wizard" forever. Could he still charm his fans while playing a different role?

Clumsy

Daniel grew up in London, England, as an only child. His mother was a casting agent and was involved in productions in the area. He showed an interest in acting at an early age and made his acting debut in a BBC production of *David Copperfield* when he was ten. Acting came naturally to Daniel. He had found something that he was good at and appreciated the escape from the classroom. At school, Daniel struggled. He had a hard time learning and keeping up with what others thought were simple tasks. He sometimes felt hyperactive or struggled to concentrate. On the set of the Harry Potter films, it was a different story. His high energy level was helpful, and his work held his attention.

Fans all over the world were spellbound by Daniel's portrayal of Harry Potter. Many kids saw themselves in this unlikely wizard who felt like an outsider. They cheered as he overcame obstacles and found power—and magic—within himself. Over the next ten years, Daniel's popularity and confidence continued to rise with each new movie.

When Daniel was nineteen, at the height of his work in the Harry Potter films, he revealed he had dyspraxia. Dyspraxia affected his coordination, including handwriting and physical movement. Everyday actions, from tying his shoes to writing thank-you notes, required more focus and time. He even mentioned his preference for Velcro shoes—if only they were more fashionable, he joked. Daniel had revealed something deeply personal that had affected him all his life. Where other kids were able to ride bikes, Daniel needed assistance. During school he often felt like he was terrible at everything and had no talent. He explained that dyspraxia added to his poor self-esteem.

Instead of responding with empathy, some in the media mocked Daniel's diagnosis. "Dyspraxia Explains Harry Potter's Klutziness" read an ABC news headline. Referring to Daniel as a klutz was ableist and offensive. Although Daniel didn't respond, it must have been difficult to read headlines that made fun of a condition he was born with.

Even some people he'd worked with made thoughtless comments that reduced his diagnosis to mere clumsiness. These flippant remarks showed that many people didn't think the diagnosis was serious or important. Despite his fame, Daniel still confronted assumptions about dyspraxia. But he refused to let other people define him.

You Want to Know . . .

What is ableist language?

Ableist language include words or phrases that devalue people who have disabilities. These words can be hurtful and harmful. An example of ableist language is calling someone "lame." Historically, "lame" was a word used to refer to people with difficulties moving around. The word described their disability as boring or unimportant. It's easy to find alternatives to hurtful words like this. For example, "The birthday party was boring."

Advocating for Acceptance

When asked for advice for another person diagnosed with dyspraxia, Daniel said, "Do not let it stop you. It has never held me back and some of the smartest people I know are people who have learning disabilities. The fact that some things are more of a struggle will only make you more determined, harder working and more imaginative in the solutions you find to problems."

Daniel himself was certainly determined. In particular, he was determined to dispel the stereotypes and become an advocate for others who had dyspraxia—and all of those who faced bullying simply for being themselves.

Daniel's experience with being devalued and mocked helped him to empathize with other people who experienced inequality. He believed everyone should be treated with respect and fairness.

In 2020, Daniel made a bold statement advocating for acceptance. He published an essay in support of the transgender community, a direct rebuttal to other prominent voices who were treating trans people as outsiders. He felt strongly that the discrimination he saw was wrong. Daniel advocated for LGBTQIA+ rights and stressed the importance of equal rights for everyone.

Life After Potter

Daniel had never wanted to be defined by the role that catapulted him to stardom. He made a point of booking other acting jobs when he could in between the Potter movies, and after the last film wrapped, he signed on to even more projects. He sought out roles that were totally different and sometimes unexpected. Little by little, fans began to see him in a new light.

Today, Daniel continues to work in film, television, and theater. In 2024, he won a Tony Award for his performance in the Broadway musical *Merrily We*

Roll Along. Though many people still remember him as the awkward, scholarly boy wizard, Daniel has made a name far beyond that. He never let his work as Harry Potter define him, and he did not let his dyspraxia diagnosis define him, either. Instead, he has used his fame to dispel misconceptions and raise awareness of the difficulties associated with this diagnosis. He has become an advocate for dyspraxia, troubled youth, and other communities facing discrimination, too. Above all, he has gone from playing "the boy who lived" to living his own life, refusing to let others define him.

CLAY MARZO

Surfer

July 17, 1989

Autism

When he's on his surfboard, Clay Marzo makes it seem as if he somehow controls the water. Clay was only a kid when he began to impress the surfing world with his radical style. However, on land, Clay had a much harder time staying in control.

In the water, Clay could be himself, riding the waves and enjoying the cool quiet of the ocean. But when he wasn't on his surfboard, Clay felt uncomfortable interacting with others and reading facial expressions. He was sensitive to noise and had a hard time connecting with friends.

Growing up, his family thought his behavior was peculiar—he wasn't interested in participating in activities with kids around his age. He preferred to stay in the water over almost anything else. Clay freestyled exciting surf moves and loved to try daring tricks that many other surfers cautiously avoided. He would practice for hours, then spend *more* hours watching videos of himself surfing, analyzing his technique and searching for ways to level up.

Although people around Clay knew he had a unique personality, not many suspected that he was autistic. Clay had great coordination, balance, and athletic ability. There was no way he could be autistic. Many people believed that autism couldn't coexist with athleticism. But Clay was poised to shatter that misconception—and to become one of the greatest surfers in the world.

Clay had talent, creativity, fearlessness, and single-minded dedication. But it would take even more than that to turn his passion into a successful career. He would need to navigate the rules of surfing competitions, not just freely perform the tricks that most excited him. He would need to stay on good terms with the brands who could sponsor him, even though business meetings and networking events made him uncomfortable. And he would need to engage with fans who admired him, no matter how exhausted he was by interviews and meet and greets. For Clay, staying in control in the water seemed effortless, but meeting expectations on land would be far more difficult.

Conquering the Waves

Clay grew up in Hawaii, where all the best surfers went to ride the big waves. He was inspired by the water and the surfers who found a way to conquer it. Clay was a natural almost as soon as he jumped in the ocean. He swam and surfed competitively, winning a state swimming title at just ten years old and earning high marks in surfing, too. Clay was doing tricks that most kids his age could not do. He was able to control the board like a pro. Anyone who watched Clay surf saw that he was something special.

He wasn't even a teenager yet, but Clay had already caught the eye of top sponsors. At age eleven, he signed a contract with a popular surf-wear company to join their pro team and promote their apparel. The company soon featured Clay in surf videos showcasing his skills and athleticism. Clay's unique way of mastering the waves captivated fans. However, on land Clay's rise to fame was anything but smooth sailing. He was curt and dismissive with sponsors, peers, and fans. He walked away from people while they were talking and missed important meetings. Some were offended by his behavior. They couldn't understand it.

Clay was known for taking big risks on the water—doing hard spins, bending his body into awkward positions, and teetering on the edge of wipeout. This sometimes backfired in competition—he couldn't resist attempting difficult tricks, even if he only needed a clean run to beat his opponents. His impulse was to give it his all on every wave, not to strategize about judges and scoring. Nonetheless his difficult maneuvers paid off and he won a national championship at fifteen. The win caused Clay's popularity to soar, but he was clearly uncomfortable and nearly agitated with the attention. He skipped events and barely spoke to fans. People began to think he didn't care about his career, but it couldn't have been further from the truth.

One of his sponsors knew that there was something else going on with Clay. He got permission to take Clay to a doctor to assess him for autism. After a lengthy process, finally Clay had a name for what was going on with him: Asperger's syndrome. Today, that term is outdated and is replaced by the term autism spectrum disorder.

Clay, his friends, and his family were relieved. Soon, the surfing community rallied around him. Clay explained that his diagnosis was a gift. It allowed him to hyperfocus on the water, understanding how the waves moved and how he could move with them.

Just Add Water

News of Clay's diagnosis spread fast. In 2007, there weren't many pro athletes who were vocal about being autistic. People were interested in him and wanted to know more about his diagnosis. Clay talked about how autism affected his surfing. There were little things he did, like avoiding eye contact in conversation and becoming overwhelmed in crowds. He took chances in the water; that kind of impulsive risk-taking is common among people with autism. Clay showed that autism was multifaceted. There was not just one type of autistic person but a spectrum of experiences and personalities. Clay also showed that autistic people could focus and be athletic—they could master the waves.

In 2009, a few years after Clay publicly revealed his diagnosis, his life was documented in the movie *Clay Marzo: Just Add Water*. He inspired the world to be more accepting of neurodivergent people. He also worked on staying in control of his life on land. He learned how to recognize social cues and interact in social situations. Clay may still have difficulties with face-to-face interviews and busy environments, but he has developed ways to manage his discomfort through the years.

And when it comes to surfing, Clay prioritizes working with people who will support and understand his neurodiversity, rather than criticize it or pressure him to conform. He's spending less time competing and more time surfing his own way, getting back to the rebellious and individualistic roots of the sport. Like so many who hear Clay's story, Jamie Tierney, the director of *Just Add Water*, was inspired by Clay's amazing skills. He said, "Clay is so good because he has [autism], not in spite of it."

You Want to Know . . .

How can I support my neurodivergent friends?

Everyone wants to feel supported and understood. Let your friends know that you are there for them and support them. Treat your friends with respect and communicate clearly and honestly. They'll appreciate your effort!

LISA LING

Journalist

August 30, 1973

Attention Deficit Disorder

Lisa Ling always enjoyed investigating. Gathering information and creating a story was one of her favorite things as a child. It was no surprise, then, when Lisa grew up to be a journalist. After years reporting around the world, in 2011, she began perhaps her most personal project yet, a docuseries called *Our America with Lisa Ling*. A 2014 episode investigated "The ADHD Explosion." The title referred to the large number of children who were being diagnosed with attention deficit hyperactivity disorder. The episode explored the condition and included interviews with families managing ADHD. It also showed how doctors tested children for ADHD. During that time, ADHD diagnoses were becoming more common, and the disorder wasn't well understood. As Lisa reported on the traits of someone with ADHD, she reflected on her own childhood. She related to some of the traits and recognized that some of the challenges she dealt with as an adult aligned with ADHD symptoms.

With the cameras rolling, Lisa talked to a doctor about her difficulty focusing. She explained that it was hard for her to retain information that she'd just read and that her grades suffered due to her lack of attention. Lisa shared, "As a journalist, when I'm immersed in a story then I feel like I can laser-focus. But if I'm not working, my mind goes in every direction but where it's supposed to go. I've been like that since I was a kid." After evaluating Lisa via a test, the doctor told Lisa that she had ADD, or attention deficit disorder, which is a type of ADHD without the "hyperactive" part. Lisa was surprised. At the time, doctors mostly diagnosed children with ADHD/ADD. Lisa was forty. However, her diagnosis answered a lot of questions and caused a sense of release. Lisa had made a career reporting stories that helped people understand one another. But this time, reporting was helping her better understand herself.

Becoming Lisa Ling

Lisa grew up in Sacramento in a family that valued education. Lisa was expected to make good grades and try her best in all subjects. However, Lisa was not a model student and had trouble fitting in. She also had trouble focusing, especially on subjects that she wasn't interested in. Her teachers thought she was goofing off in class and if Lisa would just pay more attention, she would make better grades. But it wasn't that simple. And when Lisa got to high school, the challenges continued. She would spend an hour in one class and totally forget what she'd learned as soon as the bell rang. No matter how hard she tried, Lisa had trouble retaining information and did poorly on tests. To make matters worse, when it was test time, Lisa became anxious, which further affected her ability to concentrate.

Even though Lisa struggled academically, she went on to college at USC, the University of Southern California. Lisa wanted to become a journalist just like her hero, Connie Chung. Lisa saw herself in Connie, a popular Asian-American journalist and news anchor. Like Connie, Lisa wanted to explore diversity in America and get to know people across the nation. At eighteen, she became a reporter for

Channel One News, a daily show for teen audiences. However, she soon dropped out of USC. Although Lisa realized that education was important, she decided to take a different path to pursue her dream.

Lisa continued sharing stories and people took notice. She had a knack for investigative journalism and won several awards for her reporting and documentaries. She traveled to places like Iraq and Afghanistan to cover news stories. She soon joined the award-winning TV show *The View*. On *The View*, Lisa and other women journalists, like Barbara Walters, talked about current events and popular culture. Lisa became known for her candid responses and thoughtful commentary. Whether viewers agreed with her comments or not, most appreciated that she was honest and authentic.

Windows and Mirrors

Lisa had found her stride as a TV host and an investigative journalist. While she still struggled with focusing, the work she was doing held her attention. After spending three years on *The View*, Lisa took a job hosting *National Geographic* and later had her own show on the Oprah Winfrey Network, *Our America with Lisa Ling*. She reported on events around the world, including tough subjects that affected women, people of color, and children. Through interviews and reporting, Lisa was able to provide windows into different corners of the world and people of different cultures. Viewers got to see how other people lived and learned more about their neighbors. Her work also prompted viewers to take a close look at themselves—how they treat people and what they hold dear.

She even brought her Asian roots to the forefront by creating a documentary called *Take Out* that explores Asian takeout restaurants in the United States. The documentary travels across the United States to explore the background of Asian food and tell the story of Asian immigrants. From Filipino food in Louisiana to Korean food in Fairfax County, Virginia, Lisa offered viewers a look into an important part of American culture. She also used this opportunity to tell the stories she wished she would have heard as a young Asian girl ashamed of her culture. With her documentary, Lisa showed the world how proud she is of it.

Learning to Focus

By 2023, Lisa was back to reporting the news on network television for *CBS News Sunday Morning*. She balances work as a journalist with being a mom. She's also managing her ADD. When she feels her mind drifting, she makes it a point to do something that can help her focus, like carving out time to be still and quiet every day.

While having ADD was not always easy for her, Lisa's ability to hyper-focus has proven useful in the world of investigative reporting, with its high stakes, compelling stories, and tight deadlines. Even though she struggled in school, Lisa's unique brain helped her become the successful journalist she dreamed of being as a child. Today, she continues to connect people around the world by reporting impactful stories. And some of the most impactful stories she's reported have been her own.

MUHAMMAD ALI

Boxer

January 17, 1942–June 3, 2016

Dyslexia

On February 25, 1964, fledgling boxer Cassius Clay hovered above his opponent in a small ring in the middle of a sold-out arena. The crowd was electric, amazed at what they'd just witnessed. World heavyweight champion Sonny Liston was lying on the ring's floor. Cassius Clay, the twenty-two-year-old who had declared, "I am the greatest" before entering the ring, had knocked him out! Now, Clay would be crowned the heavyweight champion of the world. Clay, known just as much for his outspokenness as for his athleticism, had achieved greatness—true to his word. But he wasn't finished talking. After his big win, he announced that he had changed his name to Muhammad Ali and that he was a member of the Nation of Islam, a Muslim Black empowerment group. For some, his win and name change were displays of Black pride, situating him at the forefront of a new generation of empowered and socially conscious athletes. For others, what he had done posed a problem. Boxers were not supposed to have an opinion. They especially weren't supposed to speak out against the unfair treatment Black people received in America. Many Americans were uncomfortable with what Muhammad Ali would say next and who he would influence.

They wanted to find a way to quiet the big talker. But Muhammad was prepared to outlast any opponent and raise his voice louder.

Becoming the Greatest

When Muhammad was a young boy in Louisville, Kentucky, Black and white students could not attend school together. Black students were given old, damaged books and were often stuffed into small buildings that were not designed to be classrooms. Growing up in the segregated South, Muhammad recognized that life was unfair to Black people in America. He discovered boxing as a way to escape the discrimination and struggle. His grades weren't up to par, and he struggled with reading, but his teachers also knew he was a talented young athlete on his way to the Olympics. After much debate, the school allowed Muhammad to graduate, despite his low grades. Muhammad had dyslexia, which affected the way his brain processed written language and made reading difficult. Muhammad did not have much support to manage his dyslexia, but he learned to memorize passages and speeches. He didn't share his diagnosis publicly. Instead, he masked his neurodivergence with his charm, confidence, and quick thinking.

Muhammad graduated in 1960 and went to Rome that summer to compete in the Olympics. There, he won the 1960 Olympic light heavyweight medal! He learned that his athleticism and personality could help him succeed. Ali was just beginning to make a name for himself as a boxer. He would make an even bigger impact as a talker, boasting about his greatness, trash-talking his opponents, and exposing racism in America.

The Fight Outside the Ring

The sixties were a turbulent time in America. While Muhammad was racking up titles in the ring, the fight for civil rights was heating up and so was international conflict. The United States set up a draft, which was like a lottery system that chose young men at random to enlist in the military.

In 1964, just a few months before he beat Sonny Liston and adopted his new name, Muhammad Ali had taken and failed the literacy test to join the army. Dyslexia made tests like these challenging. After failing the test, he didn't worry too much about the military drafting him. But he had made a few enemies while speaking about injustice, and the United States was going to war with Vietnam. By 1966, the military had lowered its literacy requirements. They drafted Muhammad, but he refused. Refusing the draft was a crime, and anyone who did so could face jail time. He claimed that his religion, which clearly stated that he should not engage in war, prohibited him from joining the military. Religious freedom was an American right, but Muhammad's refusal sparked a national debate and the news spread across the world. Because Muhammad was known for his way with words, people accused him of purposely failing his literacy test. They questioned his intelligence and even claimed he was faking his religion. Muhammad was stripped of his boxing title, and his boxing license was suspended so he could no longer compete.

Muhammad could always outlast his opponents in the ring. This time, he would outlast his opponents by sticking to his beliefs. Muhammad went to court to defend his religious exception from the draft. His court case stretched out over four years. In those years, he voiced his opposition to the Vietnam War, spoke out about freedom, and promoted Black pride. He once said, "I know where I'm going and I know the truth . . . I don't have to be what you want me to be. I'm free to be what I want." As the Civil Rights and antiwar movements continued to grow, Muhammad gained more support. In 1971, he was cleared of wrongdoing. That same year, he returned to the boxing ring.

Creating a Legacy

While Muhammad was a world champion in the ring, his words were just as impactful. He was unlike anything America had seen before: a Black Muslim athlete whose fearlessness and outspokenness shocked those who heard him. Muhammad became so famous for his personality and rhetoric that no one would imagine that he struggled with putting together words and reading fluently. He captivated audiences with his bold perspectives and deep thoughts.

Muhammad Ali championed being different and using one's own voice to make a difference. In 2005, Muhammad and his wife founded the Muhammad Ali Center to inspire the next generation of changemakers. The center has hosted dyslexia training for teachers from all over the world, so more kids with dyslexia will be able to reach greatness. Muhammad proved that being "smart" was multifaceted. You can struggle in one area and be great in another. Muhammad didn't have to be the best or fastest reader, but he was the best and fastest boxer. He may have faced challenges in school, but he spent his adult life challenging injustice and fighting for fair treatment. Muhammad used his best assets—his speed and charisma—to incite change. And for fans all over the world, he was the greatest and most impactful athlete of all time.

ZAYN MALIK

Singer

January 12, 1993

Attention Deficit Hyperactivity Disorder and Anxiety

Zayn Malik was no stranger to the spotlight. As a member of the popular boy band One Direction, Zayn was accustomed to large crowds of teenage fans chanting his name. He traveled the world singing in sold-out arenas with his four bandmates. The band started in 2010 after the members met in a singing competition called *The X Factor*, and together, they quickly achieved global success—and teen heartthrob status. But as much as Zayn appreciated the fans' support and enjoyed traveling to places he could have only imagined, everything that came with being a pop star made him uneasy. He began to feel overwhelmed and unhappy. He was worn out from touring nonstop around the world. And he felt disconnected from the pop sound One Direction was known for. He didn't feel heard and wasn't able to bring his whole personality to the band. Zayn wanted to create music that was more reflective of his style. He wondered if it was time to go in a new direction.

As the band continued to travel, he shared his feelings with his mom. Each tour stop created more tension. Each performance made Zayn feel less like himself. At the height of the band's fame, Zayn decided to walk away. He said, "I just got to a point where I knew I couldn't go on . . ." Zayn made a hard decision, but it would take years before he felt comfortable revealing that one of the reasons for his early departure was because of his anxiety.

Little Things

Zayn grew up in England with his parents and three sisters. He was an active child. Some called him hyperactive. He got in trouble a lot, and his teachers worried that his behavior was becoming a big problem. But his parents realized he had a gift for entertaining and singing early on. They looked for ways to channel his energy into this passion. Zayn took performing arts classes and worked in school productions. He enjoyed performing and excelled in it. Despite his talent, Zayn still had a hard time focusing in school and in areas that didn't immediately interest him. His family knew he needed help. Zayn eventually was diagnosed with ADHD. Knowing that others faced some of the same challenges with focus and hyperactivity as he did was reassuring. Zayn was able to get the tools he needed to begin a lifelong journey in managing his diagnosis.

When he was seventeen, Zayn went to audition for *The X Factor*, a popular British TV singing competition. Many people auditioned for the show every year, and few people got the chance to actually compete on television. On the day of auditions, Zayn wanted to stay in bed. His mother encouraged him and helped him get to the building to audition with hundreds of other people.

Zayn passed the first segment and was allowed to sing on television. He was eliminated early on, but then he and four other competitors were asked to stay and perform together as a group on the show. The group included Zayn, Harry Styles, Niall Horan, Liam Payne, and Louis Tomlinson. The audience loved them! The boys finished in the top three of the show and became the worldwide phenomenon we know today. The band broke records and achieved awards across the world. Their stadium tour Where We Are became the highest-grossing tour of the year in 2014! One Direction was everywhere, and fans especially loved Zayn for his rich voice and style. However, behind the scenes, Zayn's anxiety was at full speed. Constant traveling and performing began to take a toll on him. Also, Zayn was disappointed that he wasn't able to be creative in the group. He wanted to add more of his style to the songs, but he was not allowed to be himself. Zayn began to lose confidence in himself. Despite all his fame and success, being part of a popular band wasn't bringing Zayn happiness.

Finally, in 2015, Zayn's mother encouraged him to leave the group. She saw how unhappy he was. Zayn had stopped eating because of his anxiety, and his health was in trouble. Zayn left One Direction and returned home. He announced that he wanted to be "a normal twenty-two-year-old who is able to relax and have some private time out of the spotlight." His fans were crushed, but they knew it was important for him to be healthy and happy. But Zayn was not truly finished with the spotlight. He went on to create music on his own, experimenting with different genres and even rapping. He finally got a chance to create the type of music that fit his personality and reflected his passion for rhythm and blues music. His solo projects did well, and he released a song with Taylor Swift in 2016. It seemed that Zayn had found a way to manage his anxiety while doing something that made him truly happy.

Changing Direction

Zayn set out to live life his own way. He released a book detailing his life and explaining how unhappy he was while traveling and performing with his bandmates. Talking about his struggles with anxiety helped many of his fans better understand him and even encouraged some to acknowledge their own battles with anxiety. After taking a few years off, Zayn released new music in 2023. His song "Love Like This" was well received by music critics who noticed Zayn's new sound and edgier look.

Zayn was able to change directions to be his authentic self. When the music industry told him that being a part of a band was the only way to succeed, he knew that he had other options. He was able to break away and do what he loved on his own terms. However, his challenges with anxiety and ADHD still exist. Neurodivergence isn't something one can outgrow, but it *is* something that one can manage. Zayn has managed his mental health by not just changing direction, but changing his pace, too. Slowing down when he needs to has allowed Zayn to stay the course that's right for him, while still taking care of himself. By choosing his own path, Zayn is now shaping his own future.

DAV PILKEY

Writer and Illustrator

March 4, 1966

Dyslexia and Attention Deficit Hyperactivity Disorder

When Dav Pilkey was a kid, he often got in trouble for mischievous behavior at school. He had a hard time sitting still and distracted his classmates with his humor. His punishment? Sitting in the school hallway. While he sat in the hallway alone, Dav came up with creative stories and doodled silly drawings. His teacher was not impressed with how he was filling his time. Dav says, "She ripped up one of my comics and told me I'd better grow up, because I couldn't spend the rest of my days making silly books."

But today, Dav is a bestselling author, and millions of kids love the silly books he makes! His first graphic novel, *The Adventures of Captain Underpants*, was published in 1997. It featured a troublemaking duo and their hypnotized principal-turned-superhero, characters Dav had first dreamed up when he was a kid. The book was a success, building a fan base of children around the world. He wrote other books in the series, and they all flew off the shelves. His mischievous duo, Harold and George, whose superpower was their amazing imagination, captured the hearts of all types of readers.

As Dav's books became more popular, some adults wondered why. Maybe it's the lighthearted silly humor or the mischief. Maybe it's the guy who flies around in his underpants. Or maybe it's because the stories came from the mind of a kid—a kid who didn't always have it easy. At age eight, Dav was diagnosed with ADHD and dyslexia, but at the time doctors called ADHD an "extreme hyperactivity disorder." His teachers often punished him for being disruptive rather than giving him the support he needed to succeed in school. When he was sent out of his classroom to sit in the hallway alone, Dav could have just sulked. But instead, he did what his mom had taught him: he tried to turn the situation into something good. Just like Harold and George, he used his imagination as his superpower. And he came up with creative stories and drawings that would one day be read and seen by millions of people all over the world.

Great Imagination

Dav didn't mind sitting in the hallways in school. It gave him time to draw and create stories. He found humor in almost everything at school, even when the teacher was going over a lesson. A simple mention of underwear was enough for Dav to imagine an egg-shaped superhero with special underpants.

He created other stories about everyday people or things in funny situations. There was a super baby and even a dog cop. He created cat kids and mighty robots. Dav kept working on his stories, adding to them and improving the illustrations as he gained more experience. Even though he loved creating stories, dyslexia made reading a challenge. Dav initially shied away from books and considered reading them a chore. He preferred comics, but his teachers didn't think they were worth reading. They had no idea just how much comics would influence his amazing stories.

However, difficulties with reading and being isolated from his peers began taking a toll on Dav. He would come home upset because he couldn't read or keep up with his classmates. He wanted to fit in, but his differences made him feel like an outsider. Fortunately, his mom supported him and wanted him to love reading books as much as he loved creating stories. She wanted him to have more confidence in his abilities and think positive, so she took him to the library weekly and continued buying him comic books. She let him choose which books he wanted to read. The extra support helped, and Dav began to love reading.

Inspiring the Next Generation of Storytellers

When he started writing for kids, Dav didn't shy away from telling his story. He speaks honestly about his challenges with ADHD and dyslexia as a kid, and how he used those to activate his imagination. He says, "[ADHD] helped me to write stories that were not boring, and my dyslexia helped me too. It helped me to choose my words very, very carefully."

During book tours and author talks, he explains how he created characters that reflected his personality. He uses his experience to connect with readers who may be facing the same challenges, and encourages readers to connect with their friends and classmates the same way. He's met kids who proudly tell him that they have ADHD or dyslexia just like him. By sharing his experience, Dav is helping shape the next generation of storytellers.

Let Kids Choose

Even after Dav became a bestselling author, some people still said his silly books weren't worth reading. In 2012 and 2013, *Captain Underpants* topped the American Library Association's list of books being challenged or banned in America.

Books can be challenged or banned in schools and libraries for many reasons, including subject matter, questionable content, or because they make some people uncomfortable. People wanted to ban the *Captain Underpants* books because they supposedly had a bad influence on children. Dav couldn't believe it!

Sure, the main characters were mischievous, doing school pranks and goofing around, but a bad influence? People complained about the books' "offensive language," mainly because Harold and George refer to undergarments so much. Some people also didn't like how Harold and George called their mean school principal "that old guy." But just like when his teacher ripped up his comics and sent him to the hallway, Dav didn't sulk. He tried to turn the situation into something good. He encouraged adults to let kids choose which books they wanted to read. He knew from experience that having choices would inspire more kids to love reading.

Do Good

Despite the book bans, Dav goes out on book tours to meet his young fans. In 2019, he created the "Do Good" tour, traveling around the world to share his books and encourage his fans and readers of all ages to make a positive impact in their communities. The tour was inspired by the characters in another of his bestselling series, Dog Man. Dav appeared in arenas, theaters, ballparks, military bases, schools, and libraries worldwide. The "Do Good" tour also supported nonprofit organizations, charities, and schools in underserved communities. The tour made headlines for its honorable purpose as well as signed book giveaways and costumed character appearances. By showcasing how books, especially the Dog Man books, can inspire readers to do good in the world, Dav offered a positive response to those who'd banned his books in schools and libraries.

Dav's positive outlook and fun stories have gone beyond the page into television and film. There's also a *Dog Man: The Musical* production that tours nationwide.

And it all started with a big imagination and a desire to do something good with it.

ACKNOWLEDGMENTS

This book is inspired by the many amazing kids (now adults) I had the pleasure of teaching for six years. I hope that you all found your own paths to success and happiness.

Many thanks to my sons for the gifts of laughter and persistence. Special thanks to my son Carter, whose interest in nonfiction sparked a desire to write the books he wanted to read. You grew up faster than I could write, but your curiosity and thirst for information always pushes me forward.

To my family, thanks for your unwavering support. I am so incredibly lucky to have grown up with a supportive and close family. To my grandmother, aunts, uncles, and cousins, I am stronger because of your support. To my mother, Denise, thanks for helping me with the kids and being so supportive and encouraging in all my endeavors. I truly appreciate all you've done. And of course, thank you to my incredibly patient husband, Jarod. You always go above and beyond so that I can do what I love. I can't thank you enough.

This book would not be possible without my incredible agent, Eric Smith (who really does rock!). You shaped this idea into something that will inspire so many kids. I am so grateful that you believed that I was the right person to write this book. Thank you for taking a chance on this slightly unorganized, neurodivergent author.

Thank you to the team at Bloomsbury, and especially editor Megan Abbate, for believing in this project and understanding the need to expand visibility for neurodivergent folks. Megan, your insightful notes brought these stories to life!

And lastly, thanks to all the phenomenal neurodivergent folks featured in this book. Your talent and persistence has inspired us all.

BIBLIOGRAPHY

Simone Biles

Crawford, Aimee. "Bravo, Simone Biles, for Taking a Stand Against ADHD Stigma." ESPN, September 21, 2016. https://www.espn.com/espnw/voices/story/_/id/17602540/bravo-simone-biles-taking-stand-adhd-stigma.

Macur, Juliet. "Simone Biles Is Withdrawing from the Olympic All-around Gymnastics Competition." *New York Times*, July 28, 2021. https://www.nytimes.com/2021/07/28/sports/olympics/simone-biles-out.html.

Silva, Daniella. " 'We're Human, Too': Simone Biles Highlights Importance of Mental Health in Olympics Withdrawal." NBC News, July 28, 2021. https://www.nbcnews.com/news/olympics/we-re-human-too-simone-biles-highlights-importance-mental-health-n1275224.

Weg, Arielle. "Simone Biles Shares the One Tool She Uses to Help Manage Her Anxiety." *Prevention*, November 18, 2021. https://www.prevention.com/health/mental-health/a38291758/simone-biles-shares-tool-to-manage-anxiety/.

Satoshi Tajiri

Eldred-Cohen, Colin. "How Satoshi Tajiri's Autism Helped Create Pokemon." The Art of Autism, August 12, 2018. https://the-art-of-autism.com/how-satoshi-tajiris-autism-helped-create-pokemon/.

M., S. "The Legacy of Pokémon for Millennials." *Economist*, February 28, 2016. https://www.economist.com/prospero/2016/02/28/the-legacy-of-pokemon-for-millennials.

Satoshi, Tajiri. *Encyclopedia Britannica*. https://www.britannica.com/biography/Satoshi-Tajiri.

Armani Williams

Autism Speaks. "Meet Armani W." Updated 2024. https://www.autismspeaks.org/profile/meet-armani-w.

Browley, Jasmine. "NASCAR Partners with First Black and Openly Autistic Driver." *Essence*, May 9, 2022. https://www.essence.com/news/money-career/nascar-first-black-autistic-driver/.

Inside Track Motorsport News. "Successful Debut for Williams with CBRT at Delaware." June 5, 2017. https://www.insidetracknews.com/successful-debut-for-williams-with-cbrt-at-delaware/.

Lee, Lauren. "NASCAR Driver Armani Williams Fuels Autism Awareness and Inclusivity." CNN, September 17, 2022. https://www.cnn.com/2022/09/17/health/armani-williams-autistic-nascar -hf-trnd/index.html.

Billie Eilish

Cahn, Lauren. "Billie Eilish's History with Tourette Syndrome Explained." *Health Digest*, May 24, 2021. https://www.healthdigest.com/419031/billie-eilishs-history-with-tourette-syndrome-explained/.

Garza, Frida. "Billie Eilish Says She Uses Fashion as a 'Defense Mechanism.'" *Jezebel,* June 28, 2019. https://www.jezebel.com/billie-eilish-says-she-uses-fashion-as-a-defense-mechan-1835 939678.

Puckett-Pope, Lauren. "Billie Eilish Opens Up About Having Tourette Syndrome: 'I'm Pretty Confident in It.'" *ELLE*, May 24, 2022. https://www.elle.com/culture/celebrities/a40093456/billie -eilish-tourette-syndrome-laughing-david-letterman/.

Sanchez, Chelsey. "Billie Eilish on Living with Tourette's Syndrome: 'It's Part of Me.'" *Harper's Bazaar*, May 26, 2022. https://www.harpersbazaar.com.sg/celebrity/billie-eilish-on-living-with -tourettes-syndrome-%E2%80%9Cits-part-of-me%E2%80%9D.

Tinker, Sarah C. et al. "Estimating the Number of People with Tourette Syndrome and Persistent Tic Disorder in the United States." *Psychiatry Research* 314, no. 114684 (2022). https://doi.org /10.1016/j.psychres.2022.114684.

Greta Thunberg

Brady, Jeff. "Teen Climate Activist Greta Thunberg Arrives in New York after Sailing the Atlantic." NPR, August 28, 2019. https://www.npr.org/2019/08/28/754818342/teen-climate-activist -greta-thunberg-arrives-in-new-york-after-sailing-the-atlan.

Farmer, Sam. "How Greta Thunberg's Autism Helped Make Her the World's Most Important Person for 2020." *The Hill*, December 12, 2019. https://thehill.com/changing-america/well-being /468091-opinion-activist-greta-thunbergs-autism-doesnt-hold-her-back/.

Kraemer, Daniel. "Greta Thunberg: Who Is the Climate Campaigner and What Are Her Aims?" BBC News, May 9, 2024. https://www.bbc.com/news/world-europe-49918719.

Lizabeth, De. "Greta Thunberg Recalls Being Relieved by Her Autism Diagnosis." *Teen Vogue*, September 26, 2021. https://www.teenvogue.com/story/greta-thunberg-autism-diagnosis -climate-activism.

Watts, Jonathan. "Greta Thunberg Sets Sail for New York on Zero-Carbon Yacht." *Guardian*, August 14, 2019. https://www.theguardian.com/environment/2019/aug/14/greta-thunberg-sets-sail-plymouth-climate-us-trump.

Amanda Gorman

Alter, Alexandra. 2021. "Amanda Gorman Captures the Moment, in Verse." *New York Times*, January 19, 2021. https://www.nytimes.com/2021/01/19/books/amanda-gorman-inauguration-hill-we-climb.html.

CBS News. "Amanda Gorman Makes History as Youngest Known Inaugural Poet." January 21, 2021. https://www.cbsnews.com/news/amanda-gorman-inaugural-poet-the-hill-we-climb/.

Doyle, Nancy. 2021. "Neurodivergence and the Spirit of Progress: The Hill We Climb." *Forbes*, January 21, 2021. https://www.forbes.com/sites/drnancydoyle/2021/01/21/neurodivergence-and-the-spirit-of-progress/.

Elizabeth, De. "Amanda Gorman Had Nightmares Leading Up to Her Inauguration Appearance." *Teen Vogue*, January 22, 2022. https://www.teenvogue.com/story/amanda-gorman-fear-inauguration-performance.

Obama, Michelle. "Amanda Gorman and Michelle Obama in Conversation." *Time*, February 4, 2021. https://time.com/5933596/amanda-gorman-michelle-obama-interview/.

Slater Tate, Allison. "Here's What Poet Amanda Gorman Says about Her Speech, Auditory Issues." *Today*, January 21, 2021. https://www.today.com/parents/poet-amanda-gorman-has-speech-auditory-processing-issues-t206441.

Zelazko, Alicja. "Amanda Gorman." Britannica, March 3, 2022. https://www.britannica.com/biography/Amanda-Gorman.

Jason Arday

Andrews, Frank. "Meet Jason Arday, Cambridge University's Youngest Ever Black Professor, Who Didn't Speak until He Was 11." CBS, March 2, 2023. https://www.cbsnews.com/news/jason-arday-cambridge-university-youngest-black-professor-didnt-speak-age-11-autism/.

Brinkhurst-Cuff, Charlie. "Jason Arday: He Learned to Talk at 11 and Read at 18—Then Became Cambridge's Youngest Black Professor." *Guardian*, July 11, 2023. https://www.theguardian.com/society/2023/jul/11/jason-arday-cambridge-university-youngest-black-professor.

Harris-Perry, Dr. Mellissa. "A Conversation with the Youngest Black Professor at Cambridge: The Takeaway." WNYC Studios, March 20, 2023. https://www.wnycstudios.org/podcasts/takeaway/segments/black-professor-cambridge.

Octavia E. Butler

Bates, Karen. "Octavia Butler: Writing Herself into the Story." NPR, July 10, 2017. https://www.npr.org/sections/codeswitch/2017/07/10/535879364/octavia-butler-writing-herself-into-the-story.

Butler, Octavia. "About the Author." n.d. https://www.octaviabutler.com/theauthor.

Butler, Octavia. " 'Devil Girl from Mars': Why I Write Science Fiction," MIT Black History Project, 1998. https://www.blackhistory.mit.edu/archive/transcript-devil-girl-mars-why-i-write-science-fiction-octavia-butler-1998.

Jung, E. Alex. "The Spectacular Life of Octavia E. Butler." *Vulture*, November 21, 2022. https://www.vulture.com/article/octavia-e-butler-profile.html.

Los Angeles Times. " 'Genius' Author Takes Sci-Fi Approach to Earthly Issues." *Los Angeles Times*, July 22, 1995. https://www.latimes.com/archives/la-xpm-1995-07-22-me-26680-story.html.

Rothberg, Emma. "Octavia Estelle Butler." National Women's History Museum, 2021. https://www.womenshistory.org/education-resources/biographies/octavia-estelle-butler.

Yale Center for Dyslexia & Creativity. "Octavia Butler, Award-Winning Author." n.d. https://dyslexia.yale.edu/story/octavia-butler/.

Camonghne Felix

Aviles, Gwen. "Elizabeth Warren Strategist Nominated for National Book Award." NBC, September 25, 2019. https://www.nbcnews.com/news/nbcblk/elizabeth-warren-strategist-nominated-national-book-award-n1058206

Felix, Camonghe. "Camonghne Felix with Bunny Michael: Dyscalculia." New York Public Library, February 22, 2023. https://www.nypl.org/events/programs/2023/02/22/dyscalculia.

Felix, Camonghne. "Math Is Magic." *Atlantic*, February 14, 2023. https://www.theatlantic.com/ideas/archive/2023/02/learning-math-emotional-trauma-bipolar-mental-health/673047/.

"Reading by Camonghne Felix." Cornell English Department, YouTube, June 14, 2021. https://www.youtube.com/watch?v=Q1guXZxSgBk.

Vinson, Arriel. "Camonghne Felix's Debut Memoir Is About More than Overcoming Heartbreak." Shondaland, February 15, 2023. https://www.shondaland.com/inspire/books/a42863403 /camonghne-felix-dyscalculia/.

Barbara Corcoran

AT&T Business. "Barbara Corcoran: How to Bounce Back from Failure." YouTube, April 25, 2022. https://www.youtube.com/watch?v=KmqylrM2SCY.

Berger, Sarah. "How This Important Skill Helped Barbara Corcoran Turn a $1,000 Loan into a $66 Million Empire." CNBC, December 29, 2017. https://www.cnbc.com/2017/12/27/how-creativity -helped-barbara-corcorans-real-estate-career.html.

Field, Shivaune. "Barbara Corcoran on Dyslexia, the Power of Empathy and Oprah as President." *Forbes*, February 1, 2018. https://www.forbes.com/sites/shivaunefield/2018/01/31/barbara -corcoran-on-dyslexia-the-power-of-empathy-and-oprah-as-president/.

Frieswick, Kris. "Why Barbara Corcoran Thinks Growing Up Poor Is a Key Ingredient for Success." *Inc.*, October 24, 2016. https://www.inc.com/magazine/201611/kris-frieswick/barara-corcoran -beyond-shark-tank.html.

Jackson, Ashton. "Barbara Corcoran Says Her Struggles in School Had a Surprising Benefit: 'That's Exactly What Built My Business and Got Me Rich.'" CNBC, March 23, 2023. https:// www.cnbc.com/2023/03/23/how-barbara-corcoran-got-rich-i-try-harder-and-work-twice-as -hard.html.

Rella, Emily. "Barbara Corcoran Says Dyslexia Was Her Biggest Motivator: 'It Takes a Lot to Get over the Damage Done.'" *Entrepreneur*, October 13, 2023. https://www.entrepreneur.com /business-news/barbara-corcoran-opens-up-about-dyslexia-feeling-inadequate/463671.

Royle, Orianna Rosa. "Shark Tank's Barbara Corcoran Says Her 'Painful' Battle with Dyslexia Made Her the Millionaire Real Estate Mogul She Is Today: 'It's the Whole Reason I Succeeded.'" *Fortune*, September 7, 2023. https://fortune.com/2023/09/07/shark-tank-barbara-corcoran -dyslexia-millionaire-real-estate-success-entrepreneur-richard-branson-kevin-oleary-daymond -john/.

Atoosa Rubenstein

Gagné, Yasmin. "Returning to the Life You Blew Up." *New York*, March 2022. https://www.thecut .com/2022/03/atoosa-rubenstein-ambition-interview.html.

Rubenstein, Atoosa. "Facing My Worst Fear." Substack, Atoosa Unedited. July 3, 2022. https://atoosa.substack.com/p/facing-my-worst-fear.

Schwedel, Heather. "A Teen Magazine Icon Is Shattering Her Legend, One Jaw-Dropping Confession at a Time. Why?" *Slate*, September 12, 2021. https://slate.com/human-interest/2021/09/atoosa-rubenstein-comeback-newsletter-profile.html.

Selena Gomez

Cohen, Li. "Selena Gomez Details Struggles with Bipolar Disorder and Psychosis in Her 20s: 'It Started to Get Really Dark.'" CBS, November 4, 2022. https://www.cbsnews.com/news/selena-gomez-bipolar-disorder-psychosis-in-her-20s-it-started-to-get-really-dark/.

Jaggs, Devi. "Like Selena Gomez, Accepting My Bipolar Disorder Means Finding New Strength." *Teen Vogue*, November 9, 2022. https://www.teenvogue.com/story/selena-gomez-accepting-my-bipolar-disorder.

Mier, Tomás. "Selena Gomez Opens up about Learning to Cope with Bipolar Diagnosis: 'I Needed to Take It Day by Day.'" *Rolling Stone*, October 26, 2022. https://www.rollingstone.com/music/music-news/selena-gomez-documentary-bipolar-diagnosis-1234618976/.

Petit, Stephanie. "Selena Gomez Reveals Her Best Friend Gave Her a Kidney." *People* September 14, 2017. https://people.com/music/selena-gomez-kidney-transplant-from-best-friend-francia-raisa/.

Rogers, Christopher. "Selena Gomez: What It Was Like to Grow up Poor." Yahoo Entertainment, June 8, 2012. https://www.yahoo.com/entertainment/selena-gomez-grow-poor-141238776.html.

Truffaut-Wong, Olivia. "Selena Gomez Opens up about Living with Bipolar Disorder." *New York*, November 3, 2022. https://www.thecut.com/2022/11/selena-gomez-on-bipolar-disorder-in-my-mind-and-me-doc.html.

David Beckham

Banfield-Nwachi, Mabel. "David Beckham Reveals Impact of OCD in New Documentary." *Guardian*, April 28, 2023. https://www.theguardian.com/football/2023/apr/28/david-beckham-ocd-obsessive-compulsive-disorder-netflix-documentary.

Frith, Maxine. "Beckham Reveals His Battle with Obsessive Disorder." *Independent*, April 3, 2006. www.independent.co.uk/news/uk/this-britain/beckham-reveals-his-battle-with-obsessive-disorder-6104728.html.

McEvoy, Colin. "David Beckham." *Biography*, April 15, 2021. https://www.biography.com/athletes/david-beckham.

Wrench, Scarlett. "David Beckham Opens up about the Reality of Life with OCD." *Men's Health*, May 9, 2023. https://www.menshealth.com/uk/mental-strength/a43834867/david-beckham-netflix-ocd/.

Pharrell Williams

Bassil, Ryan. "The Evolution of the Neptunes." *VICE*, September 26, 2013. https://www.vice.com/en/article/youneedtohearthis-the-evolution-of-the-neptunes/.

Gonzalez, Tara. "Pharrell Delivers a True Pop Culture Moment at Louis Vuitton." *Harper's Bazaar,* June 21, 2023. https://www.harpersbazaar.com/fashion/fashion-week/a44269082/pharrell-williams-louis-vuitton-debut-show/

Hart, Jordan. "How Pharrell Williams Was Tapped for Louis Vuitton: Career in Photos." *Business Inside*, February 18, 2023. https://www.businessinsider.com/how-pharrell-williams-was-tapped-for-louis-vuitton-career-photos-2023-2#by-the-early-2000s-williams-became-known-for-his-personal-style-that-was-heavily-influenced-by-his-own-interest-in-skateboarding-which-was-uncommon-in-the-hip-hop-industry-at-that-time-3.

"Pharrell Williams on Juxtaposition and Seeing Sounds." NPR, December 31, 2013. https://www.npr.org/sections/therecord/2013/12/31/258406317/pharrell-williams-on-juxtaposition-and-seeing-sounds.

Polowy, Kevin. "Pharrell on 'Despicable Me' Inspiration: 'I Would Have Never Written Any of These Songs' Without Movies." Yahoo Entertainment, June 30, 2017. https://www.yahoo.com/entertainment/pharrell-despicable-inspiration-never-written-songs-without-movies-153522830.html.

Miles Chamley-Watson

Carlos, Marjon. "Meet the Crush-Worthy Olympian Turned Male Model Miles Chamley-Watson." *Vogue*, September 9, 2016. https://www.vogue.com/article/miles-chamley-watson-telfar-runway-menswear-fashion-week-spring-2017.

International Fencing Federation. "Chamley-Watson Miles." n.d. https://fie.org/athletes/12343.

Lewis, Andy. "Force of Nature: Miles Chamley-Watson." Red Bull, February 18, 2020. https://www.redbull.com/us-en/theredbulletin/miles-chamley-watson-bulletin-interview.

Pla, Anel. "Miles Chamley-Watson" *Flat*, n.d. http://flattmag.com/features/miles-chamley-watson-2/.

Jamie Grace Harper

Harper, Jamie Grace. *Finding Quiet: My Journey to Peace in an Anxious World*. Bethany House, 2020.

Harper, Jamie Grace. "Singer Finds Inspiration in Tourette Syndrome." *Guideposts*, May 20, 2015. https://guideposts.org/positive-living/health-and-wellness/coping-with-illness/singer-finds -inspiration-in-tourette-syndrome/.

Harper, Jamie Grace. "Turning My Tics into Music (Tourette Syndrome)." YouTube, August 8, 2020. https://www.youtube.com/watch?v=b0bcAz3o6S8.

Hornick, Susan L. "Jamie Grace on Her Uplifting Song 'Marching On,' Life with Tourette's Syndrome and the Transformative Power of Gospel and Contemporary Christian Music." Grammy Awards, August 8, 2020. https://www.grammy.com/news/jamie-grace-her-uplifting-song-marching-life -tourettes-syndrome-and-transformative.

Koonse, Emma. "Dove Awards 2012 Nominees Announced." *Christian Post*, February 22, 2012. https://www.christianpost.com/news/dove-awards-2012-nominees-announced.html.

Tony Snell

ESPN. "Ex-NBAer Learns He's Autistic after Son Diagnosed." ESPN, June 16, 2023. https://www .espn.com/nba/story/_/id/37864547/ex-nbaer-tony-snell-learns-autistic-son-diagnosed.

Kee, Caroline. "NBA Star Tony Snell Speaks out for 1st Time on Autism Diagnosis: 'I Am the Way I Am.'" TODAY, June 16, 2023. https://www.today.com/health/nba-star-tony-snell-speak-1st -time-autism-diagnosis-rcna89701.

Schlepp, Travis. "NBA Veteran Tony Snell Reveals Autism Diagnosis at 31: 'It Was Like a Clari-ty.'" *The Hill*, June 19, 2023. https://thehill.com/changing-america/well-being/prevention-cures /4054977-nba-veteran-tony-snell-reveals-autism-diagnosis-at-31-it-was-like-a-clarity/.

Daniel Radcliffe

Carter, Ashleigh. "Daniel Radcliffe Hosts Roundtable with Trans Youth." *Teen Vogue*, April 2, 2023. https://www.teenvogue.com/story/daniel-radcliffe-hosts-roundtable-with-trans-youth.

Daly, Patrick. "How Dyspraxia Appears in Children and Adults—and Celebs Who Struggle with It." *Mirror*, October 9, 2022. https://www.mirror.co.uk/news/health/what-dyspraxia-learning -difficulty-daniel-28179678.

"From Child Actor to Artist: Daniel Radcliffe Reflects on Post-Potter Life." NPR, October 10, 2013. Interview by Terry Gross. https://www.npr.org/transcripts/230950294?storyId=230950294.

Richings, Rosemary. "How the Media Discusses Daniel Radcliffe's Dyspraxia Is Outdated and Damaging." The Unwritten, January 10, 2022. https://www.theunwritten.co.uk/2022/01/10/how-the-media-discusses-daniel-radcliffes-dyspraxia-is-outdated-and-damaging/.

Clay Marzo

ABC News. "Autistic Surfer Clay Marzo Masters Waves but Struggles on Land." ABC, April 26, 2010. https://abcnews.go.com/WN/autistic-surfer-clay-marzo-masters-waves-struggles-land/story?id=10477337.

Howard, Jake. "Clay Marzo Bends Time in Tube Riding Tour de Force." *Surfer*, November 20, 2023. https://www.surfer.com/culture/clay-marzo-tube-riding-indonesia-snapt5.

Roenigk, Alyssa. "In His Element." ESPN, September 7, 2009. https://www.espn.com/action/surfing/news/story?id=4437460.

Ruibal, Sal. "Surfer Marzo Rides the Waves of the Ocean and Autism." *USA TODAY*, n.d. http://usatoday30.usatoday.com/sports/action/2009-09-27-marzo-surfer-autism-aspergers_N.htm.

Lisa Ling

"Lisa Ling Reveals Surprise Diagnosis of ADD at Age 40." *ABC,* June 16, 2014. https://abcnews.go.com/blogs/entertainment/2014/06/lisa-ling-reveals-surprise-diagnosis-of-add-at-age-40.

Shoichet, Catherine E. "Lisa Ling Is Telling the Stories She Wishes She'd Heard as a Kid." CNN, January 29, 2022. https://www.cnn.com/2022/01/29/entertainment/lisa-ling-take-out-cec/index.html

Waverman, Emma. "Lisa Ling on Motherhood, ADHD and Raising Kids in America." *Today's Parent*, June 27, 2014. https://www.todaysparent.com/family/parenting/lisa-ling-on-motherhood-adhd-and-raising-kids-in-america/.

Muhammad Ali

"About the Ali Center." Ali Center, February 17, 2023. https://alicenter.org/about-the-center/.

Davies, Dave. "New Muhammad Ali Biography Reveals a Flawed Rebel Who Loved Attention." NPR, October 4, 2017. https://www.npr.org/2017/10/04/555301222/new-muhammad-ali-biography-reveals-a-flawed-rebel-who-loved-attention.

Rodrigues, Jason. "Muhammad Ali at 70: How the 'Louisville Lip' Became 'the Greatest.' " *Guardian*, January 17, 2012. https://www.theguardian.com/theguardian/from-the-archive-blog/2012/jan/17/muhammad-ali-70-greatest.

Swinton, Elizabeth. "This Day in History: Muhammad Ali Refuses Army Induction." *Sports Illustrated*, April 28, 2020. https://www.si.com/boxing/2020/04/28/this-day-sports-history -muhammad-ali-refuses-induction-army-stripped-title.

Zayn Malik

Bacardi, Francesca. "Zayn Malik Reveals Struggle with ADHD." *E! Online*, November 2, 2016. https://www.eonline.com/news/806459/zayn-malik-reveals-struggle-with-adhd.

"Residential Treatment for ADHD: Singer Speaks about His Struggle." *Discover Seven Stars*, November 10, 2016. https://discoversevenstars.com/blog/residential-treatment-adhd-singer -speaks-struggle/.

Dav Pilkey

Engel, Pamela. "Why 'Captain Underpants' Is the Most Banned Book in America." *Business Insider*, September 26, 2013. https://www.businessinsider.com/why-captain-underpants-is-the -most-banned-book-in-america-2013-9.

Nissen, Beth. "Captain Underpants: The Straight Poop on a Grossly Entertaining Series of Children's Books." CNN.com, July 11, 2000. https://edition.cnn.com/2000/books/news/07/11/captain.underpants/.

Riffs, Michael Cavna. "Dav Pilkey Credits His ADHD for His Massive Success. Now He Wants Kids to Find Their Own 'Superpower.'" *Washington Post*, October 11, 2019. https://www.washingtonpost.com/entertainment/books/dav-pilkey-credits-his-adhd-for-his-massive -success-now-he-wants-kids-to-find-their-own-superpower/2019/10/11/75b80cee-ec4f-11e9 -9c6d-436a0df4f31d_story.html.

Scholastic. "Talk with an Author: Dav Pilkey." YouTube, September 14, 2017. https://www.youtube .com/watch?v=6EETIWRh5Uk.

Tolin, Lisa. "Captain Underpants and Dog Man Creator Dav Pilkey on ADHD." *TODAY*, July 30, 2019. https://www.today.com/parents/captain-underpants-dog-man-creator-dav-pilkey-adhd -t159768.

ABOUT THE AUTHOR

Margeaux Weston is a neurodivergent author and editor living in Louisiana. She creates nonfiction stories for young readers, including *The Story of Fannie Lou Hamer, 20th Century African American History for Kids,* and *Muhammad Ali and Malcolm X: The Fatal Friendship,* a young readers' adaptation of the adult book *Blood Brothers.* She has also worked as an editor at the Hugo Award–winning *FIYAH Magazine of Black Speculative Fiction,* and as a writer for media such as *Ebony, Paste Magazine,* and The Script Lab.

margeauxweston.com